Acknowledgements

Thanks are due to the following for permission to quote from copyright sources.

Jonathan Cape Ltd: *Kontakion for You Departed*, by Alan Paton.

Macmillan & Co. Ltd and Mrs Frances Temple: *Fellowship with God*, by William Temple, and an essay entitled "The Church", by William Temple, in *Foundations*, ed. B. H. Streeter.

PRAYER AND THE DEPARTED

Prayer and the Departed

A Report of the Archbishops' Commission on Christian Doctrine

LONDON **SPCK** 1971

First published in 1971 by S.P.C.K.
Holy Trinity Church, Marylebone Road, London N.W.1

Printed in Great Britain by
Willmer Brothers Limited, Birkenhead

SBN 281 02615 7

Contents

The Members of the Commission

The Right Reverend Dr Ian Ramsey
Bishop of Durham: *Chairman*

The Reverend A. M. Allchin
Warden, The Convent of the Incarnation, Fairacres, Oxford

The Reverend J. A. Baker
Fellow, Chaplain, and Lecturer in Divinity, Corpus Christi College, Oxford

The Reverend J. G. Davies
H. G. Wood Professor of Divinity, University of Birmingham

The Reverend C. F. Evans
Professor of New Testament Studies, University of London King's College

The Reverend E. M. B. Green,
Principal of St John's College, Nottingham, and Canon Theologian of Coventry Cathedral

The Reverend J. L. Houlden
Principal of Cuddesdon College, Oxford

The Reverend C. P. M. Jones
Formerly Principal of Chichester Theological College

J. R. Lucas
Fellow of Merton College, Oxford

The Reverend Dr J. T. Macquarrie
Lady Margaret Professor of Divinity and Canon of Christ Church, Oxford

The Right Reverend Hugh Montefiore
Bishop of Kingston-upon-Thames

The Reverend D. E. Nineham
Warden of Keble College, Oxford

The Reverend Dr J. I. Packer
Principal of Tyndale Hall, Bristol

Dr A. R. Peacocke
Fellow of St Peter's College, Oxford

The Reverend H. E. Root
Canon Theologian of Winchester and Professor of Theology in the
University of Southampton

The Reverend Dr H. E. W. Turner
Canon of Durham and van Mildert Professor of Theology in the
University of Durham

The Reverend M. F. Wiles
Canon of Christ Church and Regius Professor of Divinity in the
University of Oxford

The Venerable M. C. Perry
Archdeacon of Durham: *Secretary*

Chairman's Note

On behalf of the Archbishops I would like to express the gratitude of the Commission to the Reverend Canon D. E. Jenkins, who resigned from the Commission in June 1969 on his move to Geneva, and to Professors Henry Chadwick, Ninian Smart, and John Tinsley, who resigned in October 1969 owing to the pressure of other duties. They have given the Commission much help over the past three years and were present during the earlier part of the period when the subject of this report was being discussed by the Commission. Canon Jenkins' place was taken by Mr Houlden and the other three places by Professor Davies, Professor Macquarrie, and Dr Peacocke. Professor Macquarrie was unable to attend meetings of the Commission until after this report had gone to press, and Professor Davies and Dr Peacocke were not appointed until the report was at a fairly advanced stage of drafting. Had they been present at the earlier stages of discussion, it is likely that they would have wanted to give this report a different shape and emphasis; but with this proviso expressed, they are happy to associate themselves with the rest of the Commission in presenting it as it stands. Professor Evans was out of the country during the final stages of the drafting of the report.

The Commission also wishes to place on record its gratitude to Professor H. H. Price and Dr R. H. Thouless, who gave advice on Appendix 1 of this report, and to the Reverend Roger Beckwith who contributed a considerable amount of material for use in the catena of illustrative passages which has been selected and compiled by the Reverend A. M. Allchin and which constitutes Appendix 2.

IAN DUNELM:

To the Archbishops of Canterbury and York

Your Graces,

We have been asked to prepare this study of prayer in relation to those who have died, in order to provide a background against which the Church of England can agree upon the forms of such prayers for use in its public services. We have made it as thorough, responsible, and well-disciplined a discussion as time allowed.

As our report will make clear, we have discovered an area of common ground far greater than we could ever have initially supposed possible. This is partly because we have agreed that the basis of all prayer is a fellowship with God and one another, so that prayer is (at least in part) an expression and instrument of communion and solidarity; partly because we are all agreed that there should be considerable theological reserve in speaking of the condition of those who have died; and partly because we all realize that in this area of theology there is an acknowledged lack of definitive criteria.

In these circumstances, there must be a considerable liberty in both doctrine and practice allowed to individual consciences. The status within the Church of England both of those who find the practice of prayers for the dead theologically acceptable and appropriate, and those who do not, is, of course, not called into question.

We are happy to think that it is because of these broad areas of agreement that we have all been able to agree on forms of prayer which, though they may seem to some to be lacking in specificity, nevertheless represent an important advance in being, as they are, unitive. For this is a context which has for long been divisive and where past history might well have led us to expect sheer deadlock between prepared positions. We commend to the Church the forms suggested here as ones which, after long discussion and the consideration of many alternatives, have been accepted by all members of the Commission. We are confident, therefore, that those who care about the peace and unity of Christ's Church will see the value of using these forms in preference to others which do not command this wide assent.

At the same time, we would be lacking in integrity if such satisfaction as we have been allowed to express—a satisfaction in being able to take the heat out of past controversies—were to conceal an unease of which some of us have become increasingly aware in the course of our discussions. As we say in paragraph 11 of our report, we are conscious of being "in a cultural situation where the very existence and nature of God are subjects of lively controversy", and urgently demand the attention of Christian thinkers. That is not to deny in any way the importance of Christian prayer and the Christian hope for human destiny, of which this subject is a limited aspect. Nevertheless, many members of the Commission incline to the belief that the doctrinal responsibility which it is anxious both to practice and to foster ought to be exercised in relation to more urgent and important issues than traditional rivalries in areas of speculative theology, whose notoriety largely derives from their divisive power in days past.

IAN DUNELM:
Chairman

*30 September 1970*On behalf of the Commission

The Communion of Saints

1 At the heart of Christian faith and worship and life stands the mystery of the cross and resurrection of the Lord Jesus, his triumph over death by death. To be a believer means in some way to be drawn into his dying and resurrection from the dead. This faith in the victory of Christ has given to Christian people a sure confidence in the face of death and a sure confidence about their relationship with the departed[1] in Christ. Of itself, this confidence does not remove the many uncertainties which arise when men begin to think of the departed and their condition. There are enigmas of which Christian minds have been aware since the very first days of the Church (witness 1 Thess. 4). But this faith does take from our attitude that fear and anxiety, that inconsolable grief, which mark much of man's reaction in the presence of death.

2 For this reason, there is a characteristic Christian attitude towards death which is shared by those who differ on other questions. Although the seriousness and decisive character of death can never be minimized, its power has been broken and its terror taken away. Those who are in Christ remain united with one another in him, even when death has divided them. The fellowship of the Holy Spirit is not broken. God is a God not of the dead but of the living, for all live to him.

3 In approaching the controversial questions with which this report is concerned, it is important to see them in a proper perspective. They are only elements within a much larger area of shared conviction. All Christians are agreed that whatever fellowship we have with the departed is a fellowship in God. The basic

[1]The Commission is not much enamoured of the common circumlocution "the departed" and would prefer everywhere to use words or phrases such as "the dead" or "those who have died in Christ"; but frequently in this report (and often for purely stylistic reasons) the unwanted word will appear. For this the Commission apologizes in advance.

15

attitude of confidence about them is grounded in our faith in the God who has raised Jesus from the dead, and does not depend on the results of an anxious and obsessive investigation into their present condition. As regards prayer and the dead, all who have prepared this report are agreed that we should praise and thank God for his grace and goodness revealed in the lives of those who have been his servants, and for the reality of our fellowship in Christ with them. It is only on the question of whether or not this praise should extend into prayers of petition and intercession for them that the division comes. And here again, despite the difference of conviction, there is an underlying unity of intention. Those of us who believe and practise prayer for the departed do so as an expression of our confidence that God holds them in his mercy, while those of us who refrain from making this type of prayer do so (at least in part) because we feel that the restraint itself shows the greatest possible confidence in the love and mercy of God. All are agreed that our relationship with the Christian dead is in God and through Christ. We are to some extent divided on how far, and in what sense, a relationship of prayer between those divided by death may rightly be said to exist.

4 Every member of the Church of England whose assent to the Apostles' Creed is given *ex animo* declares his belief in the Communion of Saints.[1] There is, however, much room for difference of opinion when it is asked whether this Communion includes a communion in intercessory prayer and, if it does, how widely one is to interpret the word "saints" and whether the communion in intercessory prayer is a one-way or a two-way movement. On the one hand, we have the statement in the Homilies[2] that "as the Scripture teacheth us, let us think that the soul of man, passing out of the body, goeth straightways either to heaven or else to hell, whereof the one needeth no prayer, and the other is without redemption"; on the other, we may instance the Report of the Commission on Christian Doctrine, which appeared in 1938 and which declared:

If there is any such fellowship of living and departed as Christians have always believed, and if the thought of growth and of purification

---

[1]We are taking this phrase in its commonly-accepted meaning of "a communion with holy people" though we are well aware that it is probable that the phrase originally referred to "a communion in the holy things".

[2]See Appendix, pp. 68-70 below.

after death is not to be dogmatically excluded, there is no theological objection in principle to Prayer for the Departed. The question of the safeguards that may wisely be imposed in any given circumstances belongs to the realm not of theology but of pastoral expediency.[1]

5 We believe, however, that the time may now be ripe for a new look at an old problem. One of our starting-points is the multiform character of prayer itself. The matter is partly (though not exclusively) semantic. At its deepest level, and always in one of its aspects, prayer is God-directed, and therefore adoration, worship, love, and humility are appropriate. But prayer also includes the wider business of the articulation before God of our human anxieties, hopes, and desires, which form the raw material of petition and intercession.

6 At this deepest level of prayer there is widespread agreement on the propriety, indeed the necessity, of the association of the living with the departed. Our adoration of God is a sharing of the worship of "the whole company of heaven". Our love in Christ does not cease when this life ends for us or for others. Praise and thanksgiving to God for those who have died would similarly be agreed by all as appropriate and legitimate. This certainly starts from what they have meant to us in Christ in this life, their service of God and of man, but should also extend to what God is revealing to them of himself and working out in them now in his fuller presence and the more perfect understanding of his will.

7 It is at the level of petition for the dead that a whole set of problems have historically and even contemporarily been raised. Many of them, no doubt, also apply to petition for the living by the living, and in so far as this is true, the Commission hopes that the paper on *Our Understanding of Prayer* which has been prepared under its aegis and which is being published simultaneously with this report[2] may be of assistance. But they are often held to have a special force and piquancy when applied to petition by the living for the departed. For instance, when we are praying for the departed, are we asking God to do things he has already determined either to do or not to do, so that our prayer can have

[1]*Doctrine in the Church of England* (S.P.C.K. 1938), p. 216.
[2]*Our Understanding of Prayer*, by I. T. Ramsey. Occasional Paper No. 1 of the Archbishops' Commission on Christian Doctrine (S.P.C.K. 1971)

17

no effect upon the issue one way or the other? Are we asking God to change his mind as to the fate of, or the treatment in store for, particular souls? Are we assuming that, in default of our prayers, God will not do the good things for which we are asking? Or that unless we pray he will not do these good things as effectively or as quickly, so that our prayers have power to intensify or speed up God's action? Is it possible to pray effectively if one does not know enough detail about the situation involved to specify what changes in it would be desirable?

8 For many, the association of the living and the departed raises as few difficulties at the level of petition as it does elsewhere; for others the problems now begin. Nevertheless, the measure of agreement is both welcome and far-reaching. Except possibly in modes of expression, there is no disagreement on the association of the living and the departed in the more specifically God-orientated aspects of prayer. The sole disagreement lies in the theological appropriateness of the articulation before God of human hopes and desires for the dead, given the nature and necessary limitations of the Christian doctrine of the future life. It is in the light of these considerations (partly semantic but partly theological) that this report should be read.

Pro and Con

9 The case for offering intercessory prayer for those who have died in Christ has included such arguments as the following:

(i) Since it is entirely right and natural to express through prayer our thoughts and wishes and hopes for those on this earth whom we love within the family of God, why should these prayers cease the moment the person for whom they are offered passes through the thin veil which separates us from the more glorious life beyond? Prayer is a spontaneous expression of love, and, since we love the departed, we cannot help praying for them. To deny to those of us who are left behind the comfort of sharing our love for the departed in prayer is to deny a human instinct implanted by God himself. However the theologians may seek to justify such a denial, it cannot but help to weaken the hold on the rank and file of worshippers of the doctrine of the communion of living and departed in Christ Jesus.

(ii) By praying for the Christian dead, we do not suggest that we are pleading with a reluctant God to change his mind or to alter his purpose concerning them. Rather, we express a simple, trustful confidence in the loving care and mercy of a heavenly Father. We know that for those who love him he will do more either than they desire or deserve. As an earlier Doctrine Commission remarked,

all Christian prayer aims at being prayer that God's will may be done; Prayer for the Departed is not, any more than any other prayer, an attempt to persuade or suggest to God some action that it was not already His will to take.[1]

(iii) Few people would feel that at death they were sufficiently mature for the direct vision of God or for his immediate presence;

[1] *Doctrine in the Church of England* (S.P.C.K. 1938), p. 216.

19

nor would they presume that engrained habits of sin could be immediately eradicated. To hold that any Christian, even the most faithful, will be transformed into immediate perfection at death seems to many people incredible and verging on magic. It would seem that the turning of a sinful person—even of a person who desired the consummation of the vision of God—into the divine likeness cannot be an instantaneous process if human nature and free will and the continuity of the individual personality across the divide of death are to be respected. In any case, since felicity as known in this life is temporal, and a temporal situation (at least as we know it here) is a context for action and development, how is it possible to picture a state after death in which such temporal characteristics as joy and felicity, though they are posited of persons, yet have no development? All these considerations make many Christians incline to the belief that development is possible after death; if this is so, then prayers of intercession are in order. We could be forbidden to intercede only if the situation towards which our prayers were directed was unalterably static. Prayers for the development of the departed need not imply any doubt on our part as to the outcome of their further pilgrimage, as though they could be assured of salvation at the time of death and yet lose their way thereafter. They may rather be prayers for a deepening of character and for a greater maturity of personality. Nor need prayers for light and peace imply a present lack. We may always pray for an increase (or even a continuance) of what is currently being enjoyed by the people for whom we pray.

(iv) If we grant the possibility of continued growth in the knowledge and love of God after death, there is no reason why the practice of prayers for the Christian dead should contradict the doctrines of assurance or of justification by faith alone. When a person comes into a vital personal relationship with God, knows himself to be justified, and knows that God cannot let him go, we may still pray for good things for that person during the time of his Christian pilgrimage here on earth without denying the doctrines either of assurance or of justification. If this is true in the case of praying for a justified person on this earth, it is none the less true of praying for him after his death.

(v) Although prayers for the departed are often construed in terms of necessity and profit, this misrepresents the emphasis of Christian prayer. To inquire whether it is necessary or profitable to pray for the departed or to ask for the prayers of the saints is to put the question wrongly. Prayer is never a matter of necessity or profit; it is a matter of love. It is a free and personal act in which man rises up into the freedom of God and becomes truly a fellow-worker with him. To pray for the Christian dead (and even to claim their prayers on our behalf) is on this view a natural expression of our solidarity in the redemptive and reconciling love of Christ. In the Spirit, through Christ, we are made free to remember and love the departed, in a trusting love which overcomes the barrier of death.

(vi) The communion which we have in Christ both with those in this world and with those beyond is a communion in the love of God. Any relationship which we have with the departed must therefore be grounded in that love, and expressive of it. That love is revealed in Christ and active in the hearts and minds of men through the work of the Holy Spirit. Our relationship with the departed must also therefore be christocentric and filled with the Spirit. Any cult of the saints, or prayer for the departed, which compromised that primal reality, would (from the Christian point of view) have to be considered unworthy. But the love of Christ and the activity of the Spirit have been present in very many individuals throughout history. If our true Christocentrism becomes an exclusive Christomonism,[1] we deprive Christ of the very glory we seek to give him. He is the first-born among many brethren. The individual Christian in his private prayers, like the whole Christian community in its public liturgy, is thus free to remember before God, to pray with and for, those who have departed this life in the faith and fear of God, and to ask them to do the same in return. The Communion of Saints is a communion in and through the love of Christ in the Holy Spirit. We are thus united primarily in prayer to the one God, and then in mutual prayer for one another. All the departed in Christ pray for us, and we pray for all of them; there ought here to be no hard-and-fast line between the "saints" in the sense of "those who have received canonization" and the "saints" in the New Testament sense of the word, where it refers to all Christians.

---

[1] In this report, *Christocentrism* describes an attitude in which prayer and faith are centred upon Christ, and *Christomonism* (for which see paragraph 10 (vi) below) refers to an attitude which concentrates on Christ *alone*, and is characteristic of the faith and prayer of the Reformation.

10 The case against prayers for the dead has included such arguments as the following:

(i) To pray for the Christian dead is unnecessary and doctrinally misleading; to pray for others who have died is improper. This life is the time for making an irrevocable choice either for God or against him. No change of direction is possible after death. If a person has been faithful on earth and has appropriated the benefits of the atonement, there is no need to pray that everlasting life and peace should come upon him. To pray that "the faithful departed may rest in peace" is therefore doctrinally inconsistent, in that it implies that they are not at rest (else why should we pray for rest?) and that they do not have peace; and, practically, it is pointless, since what is prayed for is already theirs. Altern- atively, if a person has rejected God on earth, there will be no second chance hereafter. Those who pray for a second chance are thus attempting to pray a prayer in the name of Jesus which is not in accordance with the will of God and are therefore doing something theologically improper.

(ii) Prayer for the dead has in the past led to practices which have had pernicious moral consequences. What happened at one time in Christian history could happen again, and could lead to the temptation to sin in this life and leave repentance for the life to come.

(iii) Prayers for the departed minimize and even deny Christ's victory over death. Because of this victory the Christian after death no longer needs the help given through the prayers of others. To suppose otherwise is to imply that our victory in Christ is a victory only in name—a hollow victory indeed.

(iv) To pray for those who have died is to undermine Christian assurance. This doctrine, whose citizen rights within Anglican theology are provided by Article XVII, hold that, once a person has put his faith in the Lord Jesus Christ, God remains faithful through death and there can never be any question at all as to his fate. This doctrine expresses the blood-bought right of every Christian: the right to say, "Now I know that God will never let go of me; Jesus has promised (John 10.29) that no man is able to pluck me out of his Father's hand". This knowledge is an expression not of a subjective feeling but of an objective certainty. We cannot therefore pray of a Christian, "Rest eternal grant unto him, O Lord" without inviting the question, "*Did* this man fall away, then, before he died? Where then are God's promises? And is it possible at the behest of a human prayer to bring a man back after death to the faith from which he fell away during his earthly life?"

(v) There is no means of telling—and there are no scriptural guidelines to help us to decide—whether there is an intermediate state between the earthly pilgrimage and heavenly bliss, nor whether, in the afterlife, progress along the Christian way necessarily continues along the same lines as at present. Indeed, there are many who cannot accept the doctrine of an intermediate state, since it would seem to them to imply that "going to be with Christ" involves a continuance of the same moral struggle which we endure here on earth. For these, a necessary agnosticism on such questions precludes a meaningful exercise of prayers for the dead. The future life is appropriately described as "an unknown world with a well-known inhabitant"; its secrets lie with him and nowhere else. We can safely infer that some of the conditions in this ambiguous universe which make belief in God and the living of the Christian life difficult will be absent from the life of the world to come; we can speak significantly of the fuller or nearer presence of God; we can infer personal identity under new conditions; but we cannot infer that the rules for Christian existence which obtain here below remain unchanged, nor can we infer, if they *are* changed, what the nature of these modifications may be. Uncertainties of this order make intercessory prayer for the dead difficult and, for some, even impossible.

(vi) A further point is possibly not so much an argument as a tendency of the Reformation, both in theology and spirituality. It is the highlighting of specially important features by the adjective "alone" —Scripture, faith, grace, and (above all) Christ. This may be taken either as a means of focusing attention positively on that feature or as a technique of exclusion of extraneous or secondary material. It certainly led in the Reformation period to a recovery of the main thrusts both in theology and spirituality and to a great simplification and clarification of what it meant to be a Christian. In the present context it took as its starting-point the Pauline insight "to depart and to be with Christ which is far better" (Phil. 1.23), and claimed not only that we could commit to Christ alone the present condition and possible progress of the departed but also that as we draw closer to Christ, so, and so alone, we are kept close to those who have passed to their rest in him. This may not inappropriately be described as "Christomonism".

(vii) The very nature of intercessory prayer makes it hard to conceive what is supposed to be happening when it is offered by a person on earth for a person no longer under the conditions or restrictions of mundane existence, or *vice versa*. Intercessory prayer involves a common structure of existence shared by the intercessor and his subject, at least a minimal knowledge of the situation to which prayer is addressed, and the possibility (at least in theory) of taking appropriate action towards the achievement of the thing prayed for. While there can be no defence of intercession regarded as a *substitute* for action which may be within our grasp, it can be granted that we frequently and rightly pray in cases where the results of our own action would be a minimal token only. But when we cannot begin to formulate the shared circumstances, let alone specify appropriate action on our part, is intercession meaningful?

(viii) Prayer should be based on promise. The only way we can approach our heavenly Father with confidence in prayer is along the paths he has shown us. Among the very many injunctions in Scripture to pray for the living there is not one to pray for the dead, and there is no sure example of prayers for the dead in the Bible.[1] With neither promise, injunction, nor example to guide us, prayer for the dead would appear to have little warrant.

11 The impression should not be given, however, that the whole Church of England is divided on this matter into two groups, each believing the question to be of vital importance and convinced that it has the definitive answer to it. Many Anglicans feel that we simply do not know the present state of the dead, whether "faithful" or otherwise. Consequently, while they may practise prayer for the dead in some form or other, they fully recognize and respect the motives which lead others to take a different line; and in a cultural situation where the very existence and nature of God are subjects of lively controversy, they doubt the propriety of spending too much time and energy discussing prayer for the departed. They are not clear that we have sufficient grounds to

[1]This matter is discussed at greater length in paragraphs 12–17 below.

justify dogmatic pronouncements on the matter (especially in view of what is said in paragraphs 12-17 below); in the present circumstances they doubt if God wants his Church to give the question very high priority and they believe that God will readily overlook any excess or defect of zeal, showing itself in either doctrine or practice, into which his children may be led by natural concern and affection for the departed. They would wish to stress the sentiments expressed in the Preface to this report, that the status within the Church of England both of those who find the practice in question theologically acceptable and appropriate and of those who do not, is not and never should be called into question.

Scriptural Material

12 There are two passages, one from the Apocrypha and one from the New Testament, to which appeal has traditionally been made to support the practice of intercession for the dead. The Apocryphal passage is 2 Maccabees 12.43ff. Judas Maccabaeus collected two thousand drachmas of silver which he sent to Jerusalem for a sin-offering to be made on behalf of his fallen troops,

a fit and proper act in which he took due account of the resurrection. For if he had not been expecting the fallen to rise again, it would have been foolish and superfluous to pray for the dead. But since he had in view the wonderful reward reserved for those who die a godly death, his purpose was a holy and pious one. And this was why he offered an atoning sacrifice to free the dead from their sin. (NEB)

13 How are we to take this? Opinions differ as to the main thrust of this passage. Is the writer primarily asserting his belief in the resurrection, for which the practice of praying for the dead is mentioned as an item of illustrative material; or is the incident introduced by the author, not as an *obiter dictum*, but as a deliberate attempt at providing authorization for a practice with respect to the fallen in battle which the writer realized was novel or unusual and might need some doctrinal justification? If the latter, does it make its doctrinal point too self-consciously to be of value as evidence for prayers for the dead as a normal part of Jewish practice in the two centuries immediately before Christ ("The lady doth protest too much, methinks")? The situation envisaged —those who had died in a holy war—is in any case unique and this text has been described as a "Jewish doctrinal *hapax*", though we must recognize the important place taken by the Maccabaean resistance movement in the whole evolution of the Jewish doctrine of the afterlife.

14 The other passage which has been held to bear directly on the question is 2 Timothy 1.16ff:

But may the Lord's mercy rest on the house of Onesiphorus! He has often relieved me in my troubles. He was not ashamed to visit a prisoner, but took pains to search me out when he came to Rome, and found me. I pray that the Lord may grant him to find mercy from the Lord on the great Day. (NEB)

15 It is possible that Onesiphorus was still alive at the time this letter was written, but even if he were dead, we note that he is being commended to the mercy of God, and the thrust of the prayer is completely eschatological. It does not appear how the prayer is related to the present state of Onesiphorus in the interim between his death and the *parousia,* and there is certainly no hint of a doctrine of gradual growth towards perfection for which prayers were thought to be appropriate.

16 Other passages of Scripture which might have relevance to the practice of praying for the dead speak to us only indirectly. The parable of the rich man and Lazarus might be held to show that our Lord's thinking included as a natural and intelligible factor the idea of the departed praying for the living, though there is no encouragement given to us to expect that such a prayer can have any effects. But it has long been recognized as hazardous to make doctrinal deductions from the incidental "stage-machinery" of a parable, and in particular to deduce too much from the parable of Dives and Lazarus. Similarly, some hold that the Apocalypse gives support to the idea of the departed praying for us—for example, the prayer in Revelation 6.9ff made by the souls under the altar; but this may mean no more than that those martyred for Christ are forswearing personal vengeance and (see the similar imagery in Lev. 17.11) that their innocent death cried out for the ultimate justice of God in the final Day. Finally, some have held that the very mention of "baptism for the dead" in 1 Corinthians 15.29 shows that Paul does not express disapproval of the idea that prayer might be used to affect the status before God of the unbelieving departed; but the multitude of interpretations of what really *was* the practice obliquely referred to in that verse is so notorious that its value for the present controversy is doubtful.

17 There is therefore no explicit and certain example of prayer for the dead, or of the dead praying for us, in the New Testament. The earliest clear example occurs towards the middle of the second century, after which the practice became increasingly widespread. We turn therefore to look at the history of the practice in the Christian Church, from the early Fathers onwards.

Prayer for the Dead in the Early Church

18 The mid-second-century example referred to in the previous paragraph occurs in a work of popular provenance, the *Acts of Paul and Thecla*, where Thecla prays that God will grant eternal life to the dead daughter of her hostess (ch. 29). Somewhat similarly, in the early third-century *Passion of Perpetua* (ch. 2), Perpetua in prison and awaiting martyrdom prays for her long-dead baby brother Dinocrates, who is represented as being delivered from torment as a result.

19 The earliest references to the practice in the writings of the Fathers are to be found in the work of Tertullian (*c*.160–*c*.220). In *de Monogamia* 10, he tells us that a widow prays for the soul of her departed husband, imploring refreshment for him, and a place in the first resurrection. Such prayers are taken for granted by him and used as one of his arguments against second marriages; a widower who marries again will be in the embarrassing position of still praying for his first wife (*Exh. Cast.* 11). In *de Corona* 3, where he is enumerating liturgical practices which are not, indeed, warranted by Scripture but are nevertheless customs universally observed in the Church, he includes offerings for the dead, which doubtless includes prayers, on their anniversaries.

20 Cyprian (*ob.* 258) is the first man to attest the link between these prayers and the mention of the dead man's name at the Eucharist (*Ep.* 1.2). Such commemoration is taken for granted as a constant and regular feature in early liturgies from the fourth century onwards. It is evident that there were also criticisms of the practice from this period, since several of the Fathers find it necessary to deal with the objections of those who are opposed to it. The author of the *Mystagogical Catecheses*,[1] for example, has to answer sceptics who ask what good prayer does for the souls of the departed, whether they died in a state of sin or not (*Cat. Myst.* 5.10).

21 Inscriptions on gravestones provide many instances of commendatory formulas, normally in the general form *in pace* or *pax tecum* (both of which could either be a confident statement or a petition, though perhaps this distinction should not be made too precisely) or *vivas in pace*, which can only be a prayer. None of these inscriptions, however, can be confidently dated much before A.D. 200.

22 From the third century onwards, inscriptions become frequent, and to the prayers that the departed may be in the peace of God are added others: "May he be with God", "May he be in God's hands". Sometimes there is a specific petition for forgiveness, "Begging forgiveness for his many sins". A reciprocity of prayer between the living and the Christian dead seems to be assumed. "Anatolius, our first-born, ours for a little while, pray for us."[2] The same faith finds expression in the liturgical texts of the third and fourth centuries. Again the petitions are usually simple and general: "Remember too, all those who are fallen asleep in hope of the resurrection unto eternal life and give them rest where the light of thy countenance shineth."[3] Sometimes there is a specific mention of judgement: "We offer the sacrifice for our fathers and brethren in the true faith who are now dead. Cover them on the day of judgment with thy divine glory. Call them not into account, for no man living is innocent before thee. Of all who have appeared on earth one alone was without sin, thy Son Jesus Christ our Lord, who is the great means of atonement for our race. Through him it is that we have hope to find mercy and forgiveness of sin, for ourselves and for them."[4] It is noteworthy that in the early liturgies prayer is offered for all the departed, including the patriarchs and prophets, the apostles and

---

[1]Probably Cyril of Jerusalem (*c.* 315–86) but possibly John of Jerusalem (*fl.* 386–417).

[2]For these and other examples, see Adalbert Hamman (ed.), *Early Christian Prayers* (London 1961).

[3]Liturgy of St John Chrysostom, the text still in use in the Orthodox Churches.

[4]Liturgy of the Twelve Apostles.

martyrs, and that it is assumed that they are praying for us. Such prayers have been and are universal in all the Eastern Churches and have remained constant in the rites of the Latin Church. They antedate and are independent of particular theories about the state of the departed.

c

Prayer for the Dead from
the Fathers to the Present Day

23 In the West, Christian thought and practice in the matter of
prayer for the dead has developed in close correlation with beliefs
about purgatory. Thoughts of further sanctification after death
through a fiery purging go back to Clement (*c.* 150–*c.* 215) and
Origen (*c.* 185–*c.* 254)[1] and were later endorsed by the vast
authority of Augustine (354-430) and Gregory the Great (*c.* 540-
604). In the sixth century began the momentous shift in pastoral
practice from public confession and absolution after penance to
private confession and absolution before penance, and this led
to the medieval idea of purgatory as the place where the tariff
of temporal suffering imposed by God on the remitting of venial
sins, as yet unpaid, would be worked off. Aquinas (*c.* 1225-74)
saw purgatory in these terms, and taught that the offering of
prayers and masses by the faithful on behalf of those in purgatory
could shorten their confinement: a view endorsed by Session 25
of the Council of Trent in 1563. Post-Tridentine Roman theology
has regularly presented purgatory as involving both expiatory and
purifying suffering, though, at the present time, thought on the
subject in the Roman Catholic Church appears to be more free.

24 The Reformers did not question the presuppositions of the
medieval discussions. They assumed the rightness of construing
man's relation with God in legal and juridical categories, but
rejected the Roman idea of purgatory out of hand, on the grounds
that God's free gift of eternal justification here and now, through
faith in Christ alone and without works, rules out all need to
expiate one's own sins after death. They held that Christians,
made perfect at death, go straight to enjoy a fellowship with
God in Christ into which penal and corrective inflictions do not

[1]Clem. *Strom.* 7.6; Orig. *in Num. Hom.* 15.

enter. To them, therefore, purgatory was an unscriptural super-stition only tenable by those who had not grasped the full meaning of Christ's atoning death and God's gift of righteousness.[1] Their condemnation of prayers and masses for the dead was a corollary of their rejection of purgatory, linked with their assumption of the decisiveness of this life for determining one's future and their observation that prayer for the dead in Christ is nowhere pre-scribed in the Bible. The English Reformers seem gradually to have come to reject the use of such prayers, for, while they appear in the 1549 Prayer Book, they were deleted in 1552. Few if any Anglicans in the time of Elizabeth I spoke in favour of prayers for the dead.

25 In the seventeenth century, all Anglican divines rejected the Tridentine doctrine of purgatory, and many rejected prayers for the dead as inexpedient if not indeed unlawful as such. However, a growing number recognized that the commemoration of the departed in the early Church did not necessarily involve such a doctrine, and came to wish that there might be some more explicit mention of them in the Book of Common Prayer. Hence Lancelot Andrewes (1555-1626) included prayers for the dead in his *Preces Privatae,* and Charles Wheatly (1686-1742) in his stan-dard commentary on the Prayer Book (1710) interprets the sentence added in 1662 at the end of the 1552 Prayer for the Church[2] as implying a guarded prayer for the departed.

26 In the nineteenth century, the teaching of the Oxford Move-ment, with its great stress on the centrality of the Eucharist and the reality of the Communion of Saints, inevitably led to a desire for a fuller commemoration of the departed. Gradually the practice of prayer for the dead began to reappear. While avoiding the developed doctrine of purgatory, a number of writers came to speak of an "intermediate state" in which the dead await the general resurrection. The events of the First World War marked a decisive point in this development, and since that time prayers for the dead have been widely used among Anglicans. They have found advocates among theologians of different schools. Most writers who have treated the subject have repudiated the view that the soul is fixed in an irrevocable and static condition after death

---

[1] See Article XXII of the XXXIX Articles of 1571.
[2] "And we also bless thy holy name for all thy servants departed this life in thy faith and fear; beseeching thee to give us grace so to follow their good examples, that with them we may be partakers of thy heavenly kingdom."

and therefore have thought it proper to pray for the dead. Such prayers have been understood as expressions of our continued communion with them in Christ: "But do not be content to pray for them. Let us also ask them to pray for us. In such prayers while they lived on earth they both displayed and consecrated their love towards us. Doubtless that ministry of love continues ... It is in the mutual service of prayer, our prayer for them and theirs for us, that we come closest to them."[1]

27 A catena of illustrative quotations is given as Appendix 2 to this report, from which it will be seen how the question has been argued within Anglicanism on both sides through the centuries.

28 It remains to add in this section that, though prayer for the departed in the fellowship of the mystical body of Christ is a staple element in Orthodox worship, and is believed to be efficacious, there is no unanimity among the Orthodox as to whether the faithful departed undergo expiatory or purificatory suffering, or indeed whether in the intermediate state they suffer at all.

[1]William Temple, *Fellowship with God* (1920), p. 79.

The Bearing of Scripture

29 Scripture gives no clear injunction to pray for the dead. What follows? Does the silence of Scripture mean that its drift (the decisive thing) is against the legitimacy of the practice? When the Bible is so full of injunctions to pray for the living, is it of high significance that we are nowhere unequivocally told to pray for the departed, or is it not? Here again opinions divide.

30 On one reading of the evidence, the argument from silence is all but conclusive. The New Testament Church was no stranger to the problem of Christians dying before the *parousia*; and the contention is that in several New Testament contexts a call to pray for the departed would be so natural that its absence is tantamount to proof that no such practice was known in apostolic times. Thus, the recipients of the letter to the Hebrews are told to remember their dead leaders, to follow their example, and to be conscious of their fellowship (Heb. 13.7; 12.1), but not to pray for them. Writing to the Thessalonians, who were deeply concerned about the lot of the Christian dead, Paul does not suggest prayer for them, but contents himself with stressing Christ's care for both the living and the dead together. He assures the Thessalonians that death does not separate from the Lord, since the dead remain with Christ, and he paints the picture of a joyful resurrection with Christ and a reunion with their loved ones at the *parousia* (1 Thess. 4.13-18). This would surely have been the ideal place to mention and urge prayer for the dead, had Paul believed this was a proper way to comfort the living and aid the departed. But he is silent. Similarly, when James was martyred by Herod and Peter imprisoned (Acts 12. 1-5), the Church concentrated on prayer for the living Peter; there is no hint that they thought that prayer for the dead James would be either useful or fitting.

31 Another school of thought differently assesses the argument from silence. According to this line of thought, the New Testament Christians, expecting an immediate *parousia,* had not lived long enough with the theological problem of the departed in Christ to be able to articulate a solution of it. The canon of Scripture was completed at a time when thought about the dead and our relation to them was still embryonic. The theology of the one body of Christ, in which the faithful living and dead are united—the theology, so it would be argued, of which prayer for the Christian dead is a proper expression—is indeed fully presented in the New Testament, but this particular corollary of it was left for the Church of later times to develop.

32 The New Testament evidence bearing on the practice of prayers for the departed has therefore been differently interpreted in the past. This depends not only on the exegesis of particular texts but also on the assessment of the silences of the New Testament and the possible extension to the departed of positive theological principles. But of almost equal importance is the wider theological context in which the evidence is placed. It could be argued that it is the very confidence of the New Testament writers that the living and departed are united in Christ which provides the basis for the practice of prayer on their behalf which is already attested in the second century.

33 Also, some on both sides of the debate might well wish to query the assumption, common to both positions as stated above, that the New Testament, the unique and unrepeatable apostolic tradition of testimony to Christ, ought to be taken as normative for the thought and practice of later generations. Whatever the value of this tradition (it would be said), it is not that of a decisive norm. This raises an issue of the greatest importance which the Commission hopes to discuss in a later report; but to pursue it now would take us too far afield.

34 The members of the Commission believe, with varying degrees of confidence, that the practice is at least not a clear contravention of Scripture; and they are unanimous in regarding it as an appropriate private practice for those who find it an expressive way of realizing the Communion of Saints and the manifest New Testament truth that death does not put an end to our fellowship with those in Christ. It is only appropriate, however, where the overall emphases of the New Testament are retained. Those who practise it must not lose sight of the fact, which prayer for the dead has sometimes in the past obscured in Christian minds, that "blessed are the dead which die in the Lord from henceforth" (Rev. 14.13); and they will not forget either that this life is the God-given time for decision for or against Christ, so that what we do here will affect our destinies hereafter (see, for example, John 8.21, 24). Full weight must be given to the antitheses of saved and lost, wheat and tares, for him and against him, sons of God and sons of the devil, wise and foolish virgins, in Christ or without Christ, heirs or aliens, which run through all strands of the New Testament. At the same time, the hope of the restoration of all things, and of the summing up of all creation in Christ, when God shall be all and in all, is also present in the New Testament (Acts 3.21; Eph. 1.10; Col. 1.20; 1 Cor. 15.28) giving a basis for the hope and prayer that in the end all God's purposes of love will be fulfilled. And a final *caveat* for those who wish to pray for the Christian dead is that such prayer must be conceived broadly, in reverent recognition of the extent of our ignorance and without over-elaboration of doubtful detail. (We shall discuss the wording and content of prayers for the dead in paragraphs 52ff below).

35 When all this has been said, some members of the Commission would still wish to press the question whether the more appropriate way to realize the Communion of Saints is not by thankful praise for the grace of God in the Christian dead, and for the certainty of their joyful resurrection, without attempting to frame petitions for them at all.

The State and Needs of the Christian Dead

36 As the Occasional Paper entitled *Our Understanding of Prayer*[1] has, we hope, made clear, it is not necessary to have a detailed and specifiable knowledge of the needs of a person in order effectively to intercede with God on his behalf. This principle is particularly important when we consider prayer for the Christian dead. The state and needs of the departed are not spelt out unambiguously by Scripture; the most we can therefore do in prayer for them is to commend a person, confident that his ultimate destiny lies in the hands of God.

37 The New Testament gives us two pictures of the Christian dead which it is difficult to harmonize. The first gives us the confident note of their being in Christ and with Christ (1 Thess. 4.16; Phil. 1.23), and the other, which can occur within the same passage of Scripture, speaks the language of sleep and talks of a resurrection at the Last Day (Matt. 27.52; 1 Thess. 4.14).

38 Some have interpreted the idea of "sleep" as a Christian myth which emphasizes the coinherence of the Communion of Saints by saying that none of us is raised on our own; we all wait until the time is ripe, so that we can all be raised together. Others, however, think that it is possible to make too much of this "sleep" imagery, and contend that there is nothing specifically Christian or even biblical about the term. It was a euphemism for death from at least the time of Homer onwards and is known in many cultures. It was presumably derived from the fact that sleep provides the nearest parallel in experience to what men look like when they

[1]See footnote 2 on p. 17 above.

are dead. "Sleep", therefore, may be no more than a common synonym for death—indeed the NEB translates *koimēthentas* in 1 Thessalonians 4.14 (AV "them which sleep") simply as "those who have died". It could perhaps be argued that we ought to drop the idea of death as initiating a sleep-stage. Whether Hebrew or pagan in origin, it is liable to obscure, in such passages as 1 Thessalonians 4.14 and 5.10, the teaching that the important thing is that, whether they are "dead" or "alive", Christians are still "with Christ".

39 On the other hand, it is undeniable that knowledge of Christ's resurrection and resurrecting power radically transformed the image of death as an endless sleep into a more vivid image of death as a transitory sleep or rest (1 Cor. 15.20). Christ can assure the bystanders that Jairus' daughter is not dead but merely asleep (Mark 5.39; Matt. 9.24) and that Lazarus' sleep is not death but rest (John 11.11-15). Lazarus and Jairus' daughter thus become images of those who sleep in Jesus, awaiting the call to life (1 Thess. 4.14-17; 1 Cor. 15.51-2; John 5.25).

40 At first sight the eschatology of the New Testament seems to present itself as a *chronological* scheme—a programme of divine activity portrayed as happening in a horizontal or historical context, even though more than one level of existence may be involved. The *parousia* of Christ, the gathering together of his elect, the total judgement of the human race with consequent reward and punishment, and the end of the natural order, are conceived as following one another in sequence. This "chronological" scheme is seen *par excellence* in the Johannine Apocalypse. But even as one speaks of such a scheme as a first approximation, one is conscious that it cannot provide a complete framework for the eschatology of the New Testament. The consummation which is finally expected has already been in some way anticipated by Christ and in some measure anticipated also in the Christian's condition in Christ in the here and now. Christians are already "seated in heavenly places in Christ Jesus" (Eph. 2.6) even if (Col. 3.1-3) this heavenly state is also a hidden one. Paul, when writing to the Philippians, envisages the possibility of his being able to gain Christ simply by dying, and his personal preference is "to depart and be with Christ" (Phil. 1.20-4). It is possible to interpret 2 Corinthians 5.1-8 in the sense that he conceives his resurrection body to be already prepared for him. Even in the Apocalypse, the chronological scheme is too rigid for its author to be contained by it. Thus, for example, the vision of the perfected Israel which includes the redeemed of all nations, although it is not otherwise due to be realized until the final portrayal of the Holy City in Revelation 21, is already anticipated in chapter 7. The final state, in other words, is not purely in the future, but is an ever-present supernatural reality.

41 In the ensuing centuries a similarly complex admixture of ideas is to be found. Many Christian thinkers in the second century taught, on the basis of an over-literal understanding of the book of Revelation, that the faithful dead would be raised to join in a thousand-year rule of Christ over a renovated earth. Others gave expression to a very different and more spiritualized conception of the soul's destiny after death.[1] The idea of the *parousia* remained throughout an accepted part of Christian teaching, closely linked with the idea of the final separation between the saved and the not saved. But in the course of time the sense of a future historical event becomes a less prominent feature of the Christian hope. The dominant picture becomes that of a transition to heaven (whether gradual or immediate) after the death of the individual rather than the expectation of Christ's return at the consummation of the world.

42 So in the course of time there developed the three-tier eschatology of the Church both in the East and in the West, in which the Church is conceived as existing simultaneously in three layers, militant, expectant, and triumphant. Nor is this a static picture: progress is possible through the first two layers to the third, and indeed it may well be that ultimate perfection itself includes the possibility of growth and development.

43 The amazing richness of biblical and patristic imagery, as just outlined, can have a bewildering effect; but we must not overlook the fact that through all this variety the Christian dead have a positive place in the total divine scheme. The prayer for them which is not an articulation of a systematized theology but the

---

[1]Earlier hints of this development may perhaps be traced within the New Testament: 1 Cor. 1.8; Phil. 1.6 (on growth in perfection); 1 Cor. 9.25 (the incorruptible crown, or reward); John 14. 2, 3 (on the future life as a place; cf. also 1 Clem. 50.5, Polycarp, *Phil.* 9).

simplest expression of thoughts of love too deep for words, is compatible with almost complete ignorance about matters of celestial chronology and geography. This kind of prayer stems from an unsophisticated love for the departed and wishes them well whatever their precise situation may be. It is only such generalized intercession which can be meaningful in the circumstances. We simply do not know enough about the afterlife and the type of progress envisaged there, to be able to itemize it in our intercessions.[1]

44 The whole Commission acknowledges that any prayer for the dead which is to gain full acceptance in the Church of England must speak only in terms of those themes which are central in the witness of Scripture, for example, our incorporation in Christ crucified and risen, our share in the first-fruits of the Holy Spirit, and our expectation of the consummation of all things at the Last Day. Some of the members of the Commission are persuaded by the uncertain nature of the case outlined above that it is only proper to pray by name for the living and that prayers for the dead, if they are to be made at all, must not be offered by name, but be cast into general terms.

[1]In saying this, the Commission does not wish to overlook the evidence of psychical research, but prefers to discuss this, as a factual rather than a theological question, in an appendix to the present report (see pp. 61-6 below).

Prayer for the Christian Dead

45 We have seen that both those who defend and those who object to intercessory prayer for the departed insist that they believe in the Communion of Saints. What kind of activities on our part, short of intercessory prayer for them, would both groups agree to be legitimate in order that we should the more realize and enjoy this communion? All members of the Commission are able in this matter to go as far as did the Reformed tradition in the seventeenth century. Baxter and Heidegger, for instance, stressed that we ought to remain in conscious communion with the Christian dead. Baxter in particular makes much of our contemplation of the saints, and our association of ourselves with them in "spirit, affection and desire" as a means of both strengthening our faith and promoting "heavenly-mindedness". A chapter in his *Christian Directory* (3.10) is entitled, "Directions about our communion with holy souls departed, and now with Christ" and condemns "the oversight and neglect of our duty concerning the souls of the blessed, now with Christ", which "doth much harden the Papists in their erroneous excesses here about".

46 Such writers (and the reader is asked to study the Anglican extracts in Appendix 2 with care) prove to us that, even for those who would eschew intercessory prayer for the individual dead, there is no need for the doctrine of the Communion of Saints to be neglected. All members of the Commission could support the use of a formula of commemoration. We can find nothing objectionable in the use of a form of words like that in the Byzantine liturgy, which, after commemorating the Blessed Virgin Mary and all the saints, concludes, "we commend ourselves and one another and our whole life unto Christ our God". We ought not to avoid all mention of the Christian dead in our prayers. When we do remember them, our prayer can be at least one of pure thanksgiving, together with an affirmation that they are in God's hand where no torment can touch them and that he is working out in them the good purpose of his perfect will.

47 Similarly, there can be no objection to praying *with* the saints, as we do in every Eucharist when the words "therefore with angels and archangels and with all the company of heaven" are used. Love, thankfulness, and joyful recollection in Christ are for all believers wholly natural and entirely commendable in relation to the departed.

48 We ask now: Is it possible to go further than this and to use the prayer of intercession for them? And is it possible also to ask them to do the same for us? And is there in this matter any difference between private practice and public liturgy?

49 The Commission recognizes that intercession for the departed is practised by many. In paragraph 34 we have already considered that this, as a private practice, may be regarded as theologically appropriate. We now go on to consider whether it is desirable to extend intercession for the departed into the realm of prescribed public liturgy. In the past the practice has been tied up with grave abuses, has weakened the grasp of the ordinary Christian on the truth that in Christ his status was unassailable, and has tended to encourage doubtful ideas about the afterlife: and it is a fact that a substantial body of Anglicans cannot conscientiously join in such intercessions. These considerations incline some members of the Commission to the view that the practice is certain to prove divisive and to jeopardize the ideal of *common* prayer, so that Christian wisdom and prudence should compel its exclusion from prescribed forms of public worship. Other members, more impressed by the authority of long-standing practice in the greater part of the Church than by the abuses of more recent times, and confident that such prayer has no intrinsically harmful tendencies, take an opposite line.

50 It is important to see what kind of arguments are being deployed here. The first position rests on the Prayer Book principle that, while the Church may freely employ anything in its worship which is not contrary to Scripture, all must be done in a way that is unifying and edifying in its tendencies. The adherents of this position do not claim that no development of practice beyond what is mentioned in Scripture is ever theologically permissible (they do not, for instance, reject infant baptism); their point is only that this particular development is less than the best, both theologically and pastorally. Those who support the second position do not rest their case on the axiom that the Church's habits in early times must always be taken as a rule of practice for later ages, but on the more modest notion that the reasons for abandoning early practice must be more compelling than they find the arguments deployed against praying for the Christian dead to be. They believe that this particular primitive practice appears theologically right in the light of the New Testament view of the Church, whatever individuals may or may not believe to be true about Christians in the intermediate state. One may maintain the propriety of prayer for the Christian dead without having to commit oneself to any one of the competing speculative options on that issue.

51 Those members of the Commission who saw no objection to extending permissible private practice into permitted public and liturgical devotion felt that the alternative course was open to the objection of involving a double doctrinal standard: a lax one for private prayers and a more rigorous one for public utterances. The distinction would look—especially to outsiders—dangerously like muddle-headedness or hypocrisy. The counter-argument was that, on the one hand, regimentation in private prayer should be minimal and that, on the other hand, it is right and necessary to apply to public prayer the criterion that it must not contain matter likely to prove contentious and divisive among the worshippers themselves. They believe that to follow such a policy, so far from being muddle-headed or hypocritical, shows a proper sense of liturgical responsibility.

52 Whatever the unresolved differences between these two views, they do not prevent the Commission from asking whether it is possible to find forms which are not open to criticism on grounds of content. To the provision of such forms the Commission now turns.

53 Since any statement about immortality is a statement primarily about God and only secondarily about man, our prayers for the departed should have much to say about God and comparatively

D

little to say about the dead. Indeed, the classical formulas (see paragraphs 18ff above) are not about individual progress for particular individuals but about the final resurrection in the Last Day. This is entirely right. It is not only easier, but healthier, to pray for the perfecting of the whole Church rather than to isolate the departed. This was the teaching of Richard Baxter (the Puritan divine, 1615–91), who would allow prayer for a joyful resurrection, provided it was offered on behalf of the departed and ourselves together:

Our prayers for the resurrection of [the saints'] bodies, and their solemn justification at the day of judgement, though lawful in itself, yet must be done with very great caution. And it is fitter that we pray together in general for the resurrection of all the members of Christ, both those that are dead, and those that will be, than to fix on the dead distinctly.[1]

54 Baxter's ecumenical breadth was unusual; the propriety of his teaching on these matters was not, however, questioned in his own day. The prayers in the Burial Office in the Book of Common Prayer are of a similar nature. They have an eschatological thrust and they do not fix exclusively upon the fate of the departed but speak of the God-willed destiny of the whole Church, both on earth and beyond:

that it may please thee ... shortly to accomplish the number of thine elect, and to hasten thy kingdom; that we, with all those that are departed in the true faith of thy holy name, may have our perfect consummation and bliss ... in thy eternal and everlasting glory.

55 If we interpret prayer for the departed as implying a present lack on their part (and not all members of the Commission accept this interpretation), the only thing we can say for certain that they do lack, in terms of biblical eschatology, is the resurrection at God's climax of history, the *parousia*. The New Testament does not give us an individualistic idea of perfection. This involves the whole Church, and it will not be available for any until it is available for all. That is why the early Christians prayed *Maranatha,* "O, our Lord, come!" (1 Cor. 16.22; Rev. 22.20; Didache 10). They looked forward to the *parousia,* and so may we, as the time when God's will would be done in heaven and earth alike, when Paradise Lost would be Paradise Regained.

[1]Works (1830 edn) vol. 3, p. 752.

56 The Commission therefore suggests the following as a form of words which could be used *ex animo* by Anglicans of all theological persuasions, although some will still deem it more expedient not to use intercession at all in respect of the departed. It only asks for such things as we are scripturally persuaded are in accordance with God's will and have not already been granted:

57 May God in his infinite love and mercy bring the whole Church, living and departed in the Lord Jesus, to a joyful resurrection and the fulfilment of his eternal kingdom.

58 It will be observed that this prayer is in the active voice and puts God in first place. The mention of God's "infinite love and mercy" is not an otiose piece of liturgical padding, but states the overarching attributes of God which enable us to pray the prayer at all. The use of "bring" rather than "enjoy" stresses the concept of movement, and of God's action as being the determinative factor in whatever is done. The prayer mentions the "whole" Church and then further specifies this as including both living and departed, because we believe that ultimate and complete bliss is not available for any until it is available for all. The formula states that the unity of living and departed is only to be found "in the Lord Jesus". It mentions the "joyful resurrection" because this unambiguously refers to a future consummation and not to any hypothetical intermediate state. The form of words is "to a joyful resurrection" rather than "through", because "through" might imply either a temporal sequence or a logical order, and either would be too specific for our present knowledge. The word "fulfilment" can mean either "the act of fulfilling" or "the state of fulfilment". It can be a liturgical gain when a phrase suggests two areas of meaning at the same time. Finally, the prayer is *parousia*-centred, but does not specifically mention the *parousia* as such, since this is not a concept likely to evoke an immediate response from the majority of theologically unsophisticated worshippers.

59 The Commission is aware that many would wish to include the name of the dead person within the prayer of paragraph 57 (i.e. "May God in his infinite love and mercy bring *N.*, together with the whole Church, . . .") in order to stress God's concern for the individual as well as for the whole Church. It recognizes, however, that others are reluctant to name the deceased in the course of the prayer, because this could blur the importance of decision in this life and the decisiveness of death. We therefore suggest a formula which makes no assumptions about what God has in store for the individual after death, and makes no specific petition for him. We are confident that the following form of words will win the widest assent from people of different doctrinal standpoints within the Church: **We commend N. to God** or **We commend to God almighty this our brother N. here departed.**

60 We are agreed that this may properly preface the prayer in paragraph 57, and is appropriate at the time of death, at the funeral, or at an associated memorial service or some other closely related service. Some members do not consider that a repetition of this, nor indeed any form of petition for the departed, is suitable for other commemorations, such as a "year's mind", since this too readily begs questions about the fate of those commemorated. Others take the view that such commemorations are fitting. While, however, there is difference of opinion about this particular matter, there is entire agreement that a form of thankful remembrance of the departed before God is both acceptable and of positive pastoral value. A possible form that this thankful remembrance could take is:

We thank thee, O God, for the life and witness of thy servant N., whom we remember before you this day.

Prayer for the Non-Christian Dead

61 If we pray for the dead at all, we normally pray only for those who have died in the faith. But there is a growing volume of concern that in our relationship of prayer with God we should also remember the dead of all mankind, including those who have died in the practice of other religions, those who were indifferent, those who never came to the knowledge of Christ, those who lost their faith, and those who died in open rebellion against God.

62 Paragraph 64 below gives the wording of a prayer which the Commission provides, feeling that it can properly be used in this context. The present paragraph sets out examples of arguments felt to be of weight by some who have agreed to this prayer. There is, for example, the general consideration that it seems inconceivable that a God who is truly a Creator and Father, who hates nothing that he has made, and who wills that all men should be saved, would not welcome the sort of concern expressed in such prayer. Besides that general approach, there is also the possibility of a more specifically Christ-centred argument which can be outlined as follows: in the Old Testament, man is said to be "made in the image and likeness" of God. In the New Testament, this idea is developed by Paul as follows: Christ is the true image and glory of God; and man, the sinner in whom the divine image is obscured, is transformed by the Spirit of God in the Church "from glory to glory" to become more like Christ, and so more the kind of being which God intended. There is, therefore, that in man *qua* man which is potentially a "family likeness" to God. It is because Christ perfectly embodies this "family likeness" that it is possible in him for the Word to become flesh, for God to be reconciling the world to himself, and for faith to declare that he who has seen Jesus has seen the Father. On the one hand, therefore, unless we say that this likeness has been totally destroyed, then in any man, however evil, there does still survive some trace of this affinity. On the other hand, in none of us has the divine image, the "Christ-likeness", been fully actualized. It is, the New Testament assures us, when we see God as he is that we shall be like him. Those who have known and believed the truth as it is in Jesus have, indeed, two immense advantages, lack of which could prove disastrous: they are freed from fear, because they know that God is pardoning and purifying love, and seeks only their good; and their conscious experience of the transforming power of his Spirit has already brought them part of the way towards their perfecting. Those who do not know, or, having known, have rejected, God as revealed in Jesus may have put acceptance of his condemnation of evil and response to his love out of their own power. Equally, there may be that in them which can make this acceptance and response; obviously, we cannot know. But if there *is* such a capability in any individual, then it will surely be helped by prayer. Such prayer is "in Christ", as all Christian prayer must be, because this implies only that the person praying must be in Christ, not necessarily the person for whom we thus seek to align ourselves with the will of God. Nor, as will already have become apparent, does such prayer imply a kind of universalism for which Scripture offers no explicit justification. Nor again is it a substitute for the active proclamation of the gospel to our contemporaries. Rather is it one expression of our faith that Christ died not for our sins only, nor for the sins only of our contemporaries and forebears in the people of God, but for the sins of the whole world. For many Christians in our day the great commission, "Go into all the world and make disciples of all nations" (Matt. 28.19), has acquired this additional dimension as they have found themselves forced to reflect on the hidden ways in which the mercy of God has been at work throughout the history of the race, and has impelled them to include in their prayers all mankind from our first ancestors down to this present time.

63 Other members of the Commission, whilst unable to underline all the inferences advanced above, commend the prayer which follows on rather different lines. They agree that Scripture makes it abundantly clear that God created, loves, and sustains all mankind, and that Christ died not for our sins only but for the sins of the whole world; but they do not find themselves able to pronounce on the fate of those who have died without making conscious response to the grace of God. Nevertheless, Christians (they would say) will properly wish to align themselves with the will of God for such people—even if this should be a will of judgement—and this is the whole thrust of the prayer which the Commission recommends.

64 Accordingly, the Commission believes it is fitting to use this formula, in which we associate ourselves with the purposes of God for all men, including the dead person:

O God of infinite mercy and justice, who hast made man in thine own image, and hatest nothing that thou hast made, we rejoice in thy love for all creation and commend all men to thee, that in them thy will be done, in and through Jesus Christ our Lord.

We do not know the ways of God with those who have died outside the faith of Christ, but we do know his saving will for all men, and we recognize the pastoral urgency from which the need for this prayer arises.

The Prayers of the Christian Dead

65 The final point to consider is whether it is legitimate for us to ask the departed to pray on our behalf. This is a matter on which the Commission is not unanimous. The majority of its members believe that those who have been active in prayer in this life, and who after death remain united with the Church on earth in a common worship of the one Father, have not ceased upon dying to pray for us who remain. But there are difficulties in arguing from this general statement to a belief that we may properly make specific requests to them.

66 Do we know what we are asking the Christian dead to do? As we have already made clear, we do not know enough about their condition to know what precise expressions, words, or orientation of the will is appropriate in their case. Whilst we have already argued that it is not necessary to be very specific in order to conceive the possibility of praying for them, nevertheless to ask them to pray for us makes many more specific assumptions—for example, that they are aware in detail of what is happening on earth; that they are in touch with the earthly Christian at his will and able to receive messages from him, whenever he is moved to send them; that the departed are able effectually to intercede for our specific and detailed needs.

67 It is possible, we believe, to make too much of these objections, particularly when we view prayer as being, at least in part, an expression and instrument of community and solidarity in Christ. Most are agreed that, in some sense, belief in the Communion of Saints involves their continued fellowship with us in prayer.

68 Seen in this context, the question is whether this fellowship can rightly express itself in our asking for their prayers; or whether this practice is one which endangers our acknowledgement of the uniqueness and adequacy of the Redeemer. We are all agreed that Christians neither know nor need among the saints a more merciful intercessor than Christ. The nerve of this objection lies in the two contrasted spiritualities described in paragraph 9 (vi) above as Christocentrism and Christomonism, which probably play a greater part in determining the two approaches to the practice than has often been recognized. No one doubts the centrality of Christ the Redeemer but, while the one tradition finds no difficulty in associating the action of the whole Church living and departed with the centrality of the office and work of Christ, the other which thinks and lives within the Reformation insight of the *propter Christum solum* is not so easily satisfied. Those who take this latter standpoint would maintain that an exclusive concentration on Christ as our intercessor in heaven corresponds to the New Testament view of the gospel and faith, whereas invocation of the saints as intercessors cuts across it; and that this is the decisive factor. Both claims, no doubt, are arguable either way; all, however, would agree that concepts such as "necessity" and "profit" are inadequate to express a relationship to Christ and the saints which is motivated purely by love. Along these lines it seems to many of us that there can be value in this practice of asking the saints to pray with and for us. It is an expression of our faith that in prayer, and especially in the common prayer of the Church, heaven and earth are united in a common worship.

69 A further danger which we believe should be avoided is that of "grading" the departed into those for whom it is improper to pray because they are deemed to be beyond the reach of prayer, those for whom we feel it theologically appropriate to pray, and those in God's special favour for those prayers on our behalf we can rightly ask. This is a danger to which the Western Church has been particularly prone. The Eastern liturgical practice of "commemorating" the saints instead of merely asking for their prayers, lays a truer emphasis upon the essentially reciprocal character of the Communion of Saints. The only person who can determine the effectiveness of any prayer is God himself. "The effectual fervent prayer of a righteous man availeth much" (Jas. 5.16), but we must not suppose that the effectiveness of a prayer is rigidly proportionate to the holiness of the person who offers it. We can rightly ask for the prayers of a very sinful and mediocre Christian for whom we on our part offer prayer to God. Many would also urge that in the Communion of Saints we should pray for the saints as well as ask for their prayers for us. In the words of the preparatory commission for the Lambeth Conference of 1958,

We desire to emphasize again the unity of *all* the faithful, living and departed, in Christ, a unity in which adoration and mutual prayer have their place.[1]

70 How specific, following this line of argument, can our communion in prayer with the departed be? Do they pray for us only in general, or may we ask our friends on earth to include us in their intercessions? Those members of the Commission who believe in some communion in prayer with the departed believe that it is wiser to make our requests in the simple form of a desire for their prayers. To do so, they believe, avoids any temptation to make the saints independent intercessors in their own right, and safeguards that centrality of Christ in Christian prayer, which we all wish to maintain.

71 In view of this difference of opinion as to the precise degree of knowledge of our affairs on the part of the saints, the Commission puts forward this wording for a prayer which should be acceptable to all shades of Anglican opinion on the matter:

We thank you, O God, for your grace revealed in all the Saints, and we pray for faith and courage, hope and love like theirs, through their example and in fellowship with them, through Jesus Christ our Lord.

[1] *The Commemoration of Saints and Heroes of the Faith in the Anglican Communion: The Report of a Commission appointed by the Archbishop of Canterbury* (S.P.C.K. 1957), p. 13.

Appendix 1
The Evidence of
Psychical Research

1 We have stated that we know little in detail about the afterlife.
The evidence of psychical research, however, provides data towards
the answering of two related questions: can we be scientifically
assured of the bare fact of human survival of death? and can we
learn anything about the conditions of the afterlife? Many students
of the subject believe that it provides a positive answer to the
former question but that the data on which an answer to the
latter has to be based are so distorted by other influences that
nothing specific can be asserted with any confidence. Other psychical
researchers remain agnostic on both counts, whilst some assert that
it is possible to provide a detailed map of the world of the life to
come. Such deep divergences of opinion on the interpretation of the
evidence show that it is highly complicated and frequently ambiguous. It can hardly be profitably summarized within the compass
of a few paragraphs.[1] In addition, it must be said that some scien-
tists doubt whether psychical research properly has any bearing on
theological and metaphysical questions, the more especially as its
findings, if accepted, run counter to many of the assumptions and
conclusions of science.

2 Many parapsychologists believe that the cross-correspondences,
which belong to the early decades of the present century, provide
convincing evidence for the fact of survival and some evidence
for the interests of deceased communicators. In them, a number
of sensitives, working (mostly through the medium of automatic

[1]For a recent and well-balanced summary, see the chapter by Mrs Rosalind
Heywood comprising pp. 219–50 of *Man's Concern with Death*, by Arnold Toyn-
bee and others (London, Hodder and Stoughton, 1968).

61

writing) in isolation from each other, produced scripts which, though individually explicable in terms not involving the survival of the group of deceased scholars purporting to be communicating through them,[1] yet when examined together dovetailed to form recondite allusions which could be read as clues to their continued activity. According to the cross-correspondence scripts, members of this small group retained contact with the earth after their deaths and maintained (at any rate, for a number of years) a keen interest in its continuing affairs.

3 The "Palm Sunday" case[2] is a particularly good example. Arthur Balfour, subsequently (1902–6) Prime Minister but then a young man, had fallen in love with Mary Lyttelton and hoped to marry her; but on Palm Sunday 1875, before he was sure how far she returned his feelings, she died. He never forgot her, and remained single all his life. The romance was only known to a handful of very close members of the two families. Balfour was a founder member of the Society for Psychical Research, and the investigators of the cross-correspondence scripts included his brother Gerald and his sister, Mrs Henry Sidgwick. Scripts which began to be produced in 1901 and continued until the late 1920s, involving four automatists working independently and in complete ignorance of that to which their scripts bore witness, contained cryptic allusive fragments referring to Mary Lyttelton. They were not recognized as such for some years, and the whole story was kept a closely-guarded secret until 1960, when all the people directly concerned in it were dead and the case could be published. The case rests upon cumulative evidence for its impact, and to quote single incidents from it would make it appear trivial. Balfour himself, who always moved slowly and with caution, came gradually, over the years, to accept that the only adequate explanation of the scripts and their inter-connections was that Mary Lyttelton was alive and communicating to him through them.

4 The evaluation of the cross-correspondence evidence is a highly sophisticated matter. The more dramatic evidence for survival, and *prima facie* the more convincing, is to be found in the com-

---

[1]It must be admitted that explanations not involving survival often appear far-fetched.

[2]*Proceedings of the Society for Psychical Research*, vol. 52 (1960), pp. 79–267; summarized by Rosalind Heywood, *loc. cit.*, pp. 238–42, and in the *Journal of the S.P.R.*, vol. 40 (1960), pp. 285–91.

munications which trance sensitives claim to receive. We may instance the case of Edgar Vandy,[1] who was accidentally drowned in a swimming pool in August 1933. The exact circumstances were never clear, since he was not seen entering the water and, by the time witnesses arrived, was already in severe difficulties. His brothers and others had sittings with various sensitives, without disclosing their names or the reason for requesting a sitting. Much uncannily accurate information about Edgar Vandy was given, some of it of a highly technical nature (he was an inventor). That about the details of his death could not be checked; some items were already well known to the sitters; but some information given was discovered to be true only through subsequent research.

When attempting to assess the value of these sittings it is not merely the repetition of the same correct statements by different mediums which is so notable ; a more significant point is the number of correct statements which were individual to each medium and which yet gave the impression of being a continuation and were not a repetition of previous sittings. . . . In spite of irrelevances, confusing details, and some conflicting statements in these sittings, it may be said that the clearest picture left in the mind of the reader is the outstanding personality of Edgar Vandy, with his rare qualities of mind and character and his great ability. At every sitting this tragic figure is described with his frustrated hopes and his distress at the sorrow his untimely death had caused his family, and his inability to repay them for the help they had given so willingly.[2]

Full verbatim reports of everything said by sensitive and sitter were made by shorthand writers and are available for study.

5 The case of Bishop Pike[3] is more recent and much publicized. He was convinced that is was really his son who was communicating through various sensitives during the months after his suicide in February 1966. But in this case it is harder to be convinced, as the full transcripts of the sittings have not been published and without them a fully critical study of the case is not possible.

6 The evidence coming through sittings with trance mediums is, however, conceivably subject to explanation in terms of fortuitous

[1]*Journal of the S.P.R.*, vol. 39 (1957), pp. 1–64.
[2]Ibid., pp. 63ff.
[3]*The Other Side*, James A. Pike with Diane Kennedy (W. H. Allen, London, 1969.)

coincidences, wishful thinking, or telepathy on a terrestrial plane between living persons; yet many students (and these not necessarily the most credulous) have come to believe that the best of such evidence contains at least a kernel of genuine information coming from a deceased person. It is highly unlikely, however, that this information ever comes through in a pure form. Ideas belonging to the sensitive herself and material coming to her through telepathy from the sitters or by other means inevitably distort the message, so that we cannot rely on the truth of information given in this way about the conditions of the afterlife, even though it is accompanied by other information whose correctness is open to independent check.

7 Be that as it may, trance and script communications contain frequent allusions to the possession by the communicator of a "spiritual body", and to progress in the afterlife. To take these points in order:

(i) To view one's own body from outside is an unusual and disconcerting experience, but one amply documented both in medical and psychological practice. It is sometimes initiated by a severe shock such as being knocked unconscious by bomb blast; sometimes it occurs during the crisis of a severe illness; often it happens in dreams and not infrequently in waking life—a recent appeal[1] resulted in the receipt of nearly a thousand cases. People who have had such experiences sometimes report afterwards that they no longer have any fear of death. They claim to have "seen for themselves" that conscious life can continue in a perfectly satisfactory way when they are no longer physically embodied, and when the physical body is in a more or less cataleptic state. But they also report (usually though not always) that they find themselves to be embodied, for the time being, in *another* body over which they have voluntary control, and assert that this "other body" has rather extraordinary causal properties. It can, for instance, pass through walls without hindrance. Moreover, in the majority of mediumistic communications (perhaps not in all) it is alleged—and sometimes emphasized—that the communicator is himself an embodied being. One interesting and possibly relevant point in this connection is that life after death (both in religious views of it and in mediumistic

---

[1]*Journal of the S.P.R.*, vol. 44 (1967), p. 130.

communications) is conceived as a *social* state, And it is not very easy to see how this would be possible without some sort of embodiment.[1] Can one conceive what it would be like to *meet* another person in the next world, and recognize him as "dear old John whom I used to know in my childhood", unless both parties had some sort of embodiment not *too* different (at any rate in outward appearance) from the ones they had in earthly life? Could such meeting—or re-meeting after a long interval of time—be managed by telepathy alone? How would the recipient *identify* the telepathic agent? Perhaps he could, if the agent produced a telepathic apparition of himself, and the recipient then produced an apparition of *him*self. But then there would be a kind of temporary embodiment at any rate. On the other hand, we are also told in mediumistic communications that there are some *restrictions* on social life after death. Those at the same stage of moral and spiritual development can meet each other quite easily. And those at a higher stage can "meet" or "visit" those at a lower stage, but not conversely. It is a bit like Victorian England, where Dukes could talk to Dukes and dustmen to dustmen; but a dustman could not talk to a Duke unless the Duke addressed him first.

(ii) The allusions in mediumistic communications to progress in the afterlife may be significant. It is also significant that the mention of Jesus often seems embarrassing to sensitives who claim to be in contact with the departed. This may perhaps indicate that we ought not to expect to learn much by this method about the future life of those within the Body of Christ; it might furnish better evidence of some aspects of the anticipated future of those who on earth were not so firmly within that Body. The fact that communications from any individual cease after a number of years at most could suggest a progress from an earth-orientated existence in which contact may be maintained with those of us who have been left behind, and in which Christ seems to play little or no part, to an existence in which earth contact through sensitives is no longer possible and about which we can learn nothing by such experimental means as psychical research puts at our disposal. But all this is pure speculation; the whole subject is full of uncertainties and alternative explanations and we have no criteria for distinguishing true information from false. We ought therefore to say

---

[1]Not necessarily a *material* embodiment in our sense; but still a spatial one, having such properties as shape, size, and mobility.

E

that those who are searching for certain knowledge of the life of the world to come are unlikely to find it through psychical investigations. The statement in the body of our report that we can make no confident assertions about the population and the geography of a future world (or worlds), or the activities of its (or their) inhabitants, remains true despite the evidence of parapsychology.

Appendix 2
A collection of witnesses
to Anglican theology and practice
since the sixteenth century[1]

The Book of Common Prayer 1549
At the Burial of the Dead (Everyman edn, pp. 275–6, spelling modernized)

O Lord, with whom do live the spirits of them that be dead: and in whom the souls of them that be elected, after they be delivered from the burden of the flesh, be in joy and felicity: Grant unto this thy servant, that the sins which he committed in this world be not imputed unto him, but that he, escaping the gates of hell, and pains of eternal darkness: may ever dwell in the region of light, with Abraham, Isaac, and Jacob, in the place where is no weeping, sorrow, nor heaviness: and when that dreadful day of the general resurrection shall come, make him to rise also with the just and righteous, and receive this body again to glory, then made pure and incorruptible; set him on the right hand of thy Son Jesus Christ, among thy holy and elect, that then he may hear with them these most sweet and comfortable words: Come to me ye blessed of my Father, possess the kingdom which hath been prepared for you from the beginning of the world: Grant this we beseech thee, O merciful Father: through Jesus Christ our mediator and redeemer. Amen.

2
The Book of Common Prayer 1552
At the Burial of the Dead (Everyman edn p. 427, spelling modernized)

Almighty God, with whom do live the spirits of them that depart hence in the Lord, and in whom the souls of them that be elected,

[1]The Commission is indebted to the Reverend A. M. Allchin for compiling this appendix at its request, and to the Reverend Roger Beckwith for generously contributing much of the material from which this selection of passages has been made.

after they be delivered from the burden of the flesh, be in joy and felicity: We give thee hearty thanks, for that it hath pleased thee to deliver this *N.* our brother out of the miseries of this sinful world: beseeching thee, that it may please thee of thy gracious goodness, shortly to accomplish the number of thine elect, and to haste thy kingdom, that we with this our brother, and all other departed in the true faith of thy holy name, may have our perfect consummation and bliss, both in body and soul, in thy eternal and everlasting glory. Amen.

3
The Book of Homilies 1563
Homily 19: *Concerning Prayer* (1852 edn, pp. 297–310)

We are evidently taught in God's holy Testament, that Almighty God is the only fountain and well-spring of all goodness; and that whatsoever we have in this world, we receive it only at his hands ...

Thus then it is plain by the infallible word of truth and life, that in all our necessities we must flee unto God, direct our prayers unto him, call upon his holy name, desire help at his hands, and at none other's; wherefore if ye will yet have a further reason, mark that which followeth. There are certain conditions most requisite to be found in every such a one as must be called upon, which if they be not found in him unto whom we pray, then doth our prayer avail us nothing, but is altogether in vain.

The first is this, that he, to whom we make our prayers, be able to help us. The second is, that he will help us. The third is, that he be such a one as may hear our prayers. The fourth is, that he understand better than we ourselves what we lack, and how far we have need of help. If these things be to be found in any other saving only God, then may we lawfully call upon some other besides God. But what man is so gross, but he well understandeth that these things are only proper to him which is omnipotent, and knoweth all things, even the very secrets of the heart, that is to say, only and to God alone? Wherefore it followeth, that we must call neither upon angel, nor yet upon saint, but only and solely upon God, as St Paul doth write, "How shall men call upon him in whom they have not believed?" (Rom. 10.14). So that invocation or prayer may not be made without faith in him on whom we call; but that we must first believe in him, before we can make our prayers unto him; whereupon we must only and solely pray unto God. For to say that we should believe either in angel or saint, or in any other living creature, were most horrible blasphemy against God and his holy word; neither ought this fancy to enter into the heart of any Christian man, because we are expressly taught, in the word of the Lord, only to repose our faith in the blessed Trinity; in whose name we are also baptized, according to the express commandment of our Saviour Jesus Christ, in the last of St Matthew (Matt. 28.19). . . .

If God were strange, or dangerous to be talked withal, then might we justly draw back, and seek to some other. "But the Lord is nigh unto all them that call upon him in faith and truth" ; and the prayer of the humble and meek hath always pleased him (Ps. 145.18 ; Judith 9). What if we be sinners, shall we not therefore pray unto God? or shall we despair to obtain anything at his hands? Why did Christ then teach us to ask forgiveness of our sins, saying "And forgive us our trespasses, as we forgive them that trespass against us" (Matt 6.12)? Shall we think that the saints are more merciful in hearing sinners than God? David saith, that "The Lord is full of compassion and mercy, slow to anger, and of great kindness" (Ps. 103.8). . . . Therefore the sins of any man ought not to withold him from praying unto the Lord his God. But if he be truly penitent and stedfast in faith, let him assure himself that the Lord will be merciful unto him, and will hear him. . . .

But that we should pray unto saints, neither have we any command-ment in all the Scripture, nor yet example which we may safely follow. So that, being done without authority of God's word, it lacketh the ground of faith, and therefore cannot be acceptable before God (Heb. 11.6). . . .

Let us not therefore put our trust or confidence in the saints or martyrs that be dead. Let us not call upon them, nor desire help at their hands ; but let us always lift up our hearts to God, in the name of his dear Son Christ, for whose sake as God hath promised to hear our prayer, so he will truly perform it. Invocation is a thing proper unto God, which if we attribute unto the Saints, it soundeth to their reproach, neither can they well bear it at our hands. . . .

Now to entreat of that question, whether we ought to pray for them that are departed out of this world, or no. Wherein, if we will cleave only unto the word of God, then must we needs grant, that we have no commandment so to do. For the Scripture doth acknowledge but two places after this life: the one proper to the elect and blessed of God, the other to the reprobate and damned souls ; as may be well gathered by the parable of Lazarus and the rich man (Luke 16.19-26). . . . Now doth St Augustine say, that those men which are cast into prison after this life . . . may in no wise be holpen, though we would help them never so much. And why? Because the sentence of God is unchangeable, and cannot be revoked again. Therefore let us not deceive ourselves, thinking that either we may help other, or that other may help us by their good and charitable prayers in time to come. For, as the Preacher saith, "When the tree falleth, whether it be toward the south or toward the north, in what place soever the tree falleth, there it lieth" (Eccles. 11.3) ; meaning thereby, that every mortal man dieth either in the state of salvation or damna-tion. . . . Where is then the third place, which they call purgatory?

Or where shall our prayers help and profit the dead? St Augustine doth only acknowledge "two places" after this life, heaven and hell. As for the third place, he doth plainly deny that there is any such to be found in all Scripture. . . .

Let these and such other places be sufficient to take away the gross error of purgatory out of our heads; neither let us dream any more, that the souls of the dead are anything at all holpen by our prayers; but as the Scripture teacheth us, let us think that the soul of man, passing out of the body, goeth straightways either to heaven, or else to hell, whereof the one needeth no prayer, and the other is without redemption.

4
The Primer 1559
Private Prayers of the Reign of Queen Elizabeth (Parker Society edn, 1851, p. 67)

Almighty, eternal God, to whom there is never any prayer made without hope of mercy, be merciful to the souls of thy servants, being departed from this world in the confession of thy name, that they may be associate to the company of thy saints. Through Christ our Lord. Amen.

Lord, bow thine ears unto our prayers, wherein we devoutly call upon thy name mercy [*sic*], that thou wilt bestow the souls of thy servants, which thou hast commanded to depart from this world, in the country of peace and rest, and cause them to be made partners with thy holy servants. Through Christ our Lord. Amen.

5
Hugh Latimer (1484–1555), Bishop of Worcester
Remains (Parker Society edn, pp. 88, 89, 186)

But yet we must beware that we go not too far. For we may not make gods of them [*sc.* the saints], nor call upon them, as we have been taught in times past; because God will be called upon, honoured, and worshipped alone: he may not suffer any to be fellow with him; as he himself saith, "I give mine honour to none". Therefore we must call upon him only, and seek all manner of comfort at his hand, which is the fountain of all goodness; and not at the saints'. . . .

And here we have occasion to be sorry that we have called upon the saints; and so deprived God of his honour and dignity, and made them *Deos tutelares,* tutelary gods. . . .

For this is one apparent and great argument to make Christ God, if we call upon him as St Stephen did; who said, *Domine Jesu, suscipe spiritum meum*; that is, "Lord Jesus, receive my spirit"; for invocation declareth an omnipotency; so that when I call upon saints, I make them omnipotent, and so I make them gods. . . .

6
John Bradford (?1510–1555) Prebendary of St Paul's
Letters, Treatises, and Remains (Parker Society edn, pp. 279, 291)

Throughout the canonical books of the Old and New Testament, we find neither precept nor ensample of praying for any, when they be departed this life, but that, as men die, so shall they arise. If in faith in the Lord towards the south (Eccles. 11), then need they no prayers, then are they presently happy, and shall arise in glory; if in unbelief without the Lord towards the north, then are they past all help, in the damned state presently, and shall rise to eternal shame. . . . As prayer for the dead is not available or profitable to the dead, so is it not of us allowable or to be exercised. For, as they that are departed be past our prayers, being either in joy or in misery, as is above shewed, even so we, having for it no word of God, whereupon faith leaneth, cannot but sin in doing it, in that we do it "not of faith", because we have no word of God for it. . . . Whereas they say, that the fathers from the beginning were accustomed to make memorials for the dead, this I grant to be true, as we do in our communion. But, to gather that therefore they prayed for them, it no more followeth, than to say that our English Service doth allow it, where it doth not.

7
John Bradford (?1510–1555) Prebendary of St Paul's
Letters, Treatises, and Remains (Parker Society edn, pp. 281f; see also pp. 294–6, 272–5, 422–30, 475–80)

So that easy it is to see that, as it is an obedient service to God the Father to call always upon him in all our need, so to come to his presence through Christ is to the honour of Christ's mediation, intercession and advocateship. And therefore, as it cannot be but against the almighty God and Father to ask or look for anything elsewhere, at the hands of any that be departed this life, as though he were not the Giver of all good things, or as though he had not commanded us to come unto him, so we see it is manifestly against Christ Jesus our Lord, by any other saint, angel or archangel to come and move anything at our Father's hands; as though he were not our Mediator, Advocate and Intercessor, or else not a sufficient Mediator, Advocate and Intercessor, or at least not so merciful, meek, gracious, loving and ready to help as others: where he only so loved us, as the very hearts of all men and angels never were able to conceive any part of "the height, depth, breadth and length" of the same, as it is.

8
Roger Hutchinson (d. 1555) Fellow of St John's College Cambridge
Works (Parker Society edn, pp. 171f, 173, 200)

The papists also bring in many gods, but covertly and privily. They teach the people to pray unto saints: to St Luke for the ox, to Job for the pox, to Rocke for the pestilence, to Sith for things lost, to Christopher for continual health, to the queen of heaven for women with child, to Clement for good beer: yea, they entice the people also to worship and honour their images. If they be to be prayed unto for these things they be gods; for in praying unto them we acknowledge them to hear us, to be almighty, to be everywhere, to know the thoughts of all men, to be a strong castle unto such as fly unto them: but these things belong only to God, as I have proved before. Wherefore they make them gods. . . .

He that entereth in not by the door, he is a thief, a robber. And why? For he robbeth God of the glory belonging only to him, giving it to his creatures. They which fly unto saints depart [*sic*] make many ways, many doors and many gods. If they are to be prayed unto, we must believe on them; for the apostle saith . . . "How shall they call on him, on whom they believe not?" If we must believe on them, then let us be christened in their names. . . . Wherefore as they are not to be believed upon, so are they not to be called upon; but God only, whose highness disdaineth the fellowship of any creature. Let us therefore pray unto him; for he is the well of water of life. . . . God is no wilderness to his people, nor land without light, but a merciful and liberal God. . . .

If the papists can shew that St Paul and the blessed virgin, and other, now being with Christ touching their souls, and in the earth touching their bodies, do now give gifts and graces unto us, truly I would pray unto them to give me some. But who is able to prove this out of the scriptures?

9
John Hooper (d. 1555) Bishop of Gloucester
Early Writings (Parker Society edn, p. 35)

What intolerable ill, blasphemy of God, and ethnical idolatry is this, to admit and teach the invocation of saints departed out of this world! It taketh from God his true honour: it maketh him a fool, that only hath ordained only Christ [sic] to be Mediator between man and him. It diminisheth the merits of Christ; taketh from the law of God her perfection and majesty; whereas God hath opened his will and pleasure unto the world in all things. It condemneth the old church of the patriarchs and prophets, likewise the church of the apostles and martyrs, that never taught the invocation of saints.

10
John Jewel (1552–1571) Bishop of Salisbury
Works (Parker Society edn, vol. 2, p. 743)

Prayer for the dead . . . although it be mere superstitious, and utterly without warrant of God's word, yet I confess it was many wheres received and used, both in Gregory's time[1] and also long before, and is avouched of Gregory by a number of vain and childish fables.

11
Edmund Grindal (?1519–1583) Archbishop of Canterbury
Remains (Parker Society edn, p. 25)

For it is confessed of all men, that, if there be no third place, prayer for the dead is in vain ; for those that be in heaven need it not ; those that be in hell cannot be holpen by it: so that it needeth not nor booteth not, as the old proverb goeth.

12
Alexander Nowell (1507–1602) Dean of St Paul's
Catechism (Parker Society edn, pp. 184f)

Master Shall we not then do well to call upon holy men that are departed out of this life, or upon angels?
Scholar No. For that were to give to them an infiniteness to be present everywhere, or to give them, being absent, an understanding of our secret meanings, that is, as much as a certain godhead, and therewithal partly to convey to them our confidence and trust, that ought to be set wholly in God alone, and so to slide into idolatry. But forasmuch as God calleth us to himself alone, and doth also, with adding an oath, promise that he will both hear and help us ; to flee to the help of other were an evident token of distrust and infidelity. And as touching the holy men that are departed out of this life, what manner of thing, I pray you, were this, forsaking the living God, that heareth our prayers, that is most mighty, most ready to help us, that calleth us unto him, that in the word of truth promiseth and sweareth, that, with his divine power and succour, he will defend us ; forsaking him, I say, to flee unto men dead, deaf, and weak, which neither have promised help, nor are able to relieve us, to whom God never gave the office to help us, to whom we are by no scriptures directed, whereupon our faith may surely rest, but are unadvisedly carried away, trusting only upon the dreams, or rather dotages, of our own head.

13
Richard Hooker (?1554–1600) Theologian
Works (ed. Keble, vol. 3 pp. 872–3)

Against invocation of any other than God alone, if all arguments else should fail, the number whereof is both great and forcible, yet this very bar and single challenge might suffice ; that whereas God hath in Scripture delivered us so many patterns for imitation when we

[1] i.e. Gregory the Great.

pray, yea, framed ready to our hands in a manner all, for suits and supplications, which our condition of life on earth may at any time need, there is not one, no not one to be found, directed unto angels, saints, or any, saving God alone. So that, if in such cases as this we hold it safest to be led by the best examples that have gone before, when we see what Noah, what Abraham, what Moses, what David, what Daniel, and the rest did; what form of prayer Christ himself likewise taught his Church, and what his blessed Apostles did practise; who can doubt but the way for us to pray so as we may undoubtedly be accepted, is by conforming our prayers to theirs, whose supplications we know were acceptable?

14
Lancelot Andrewes (1555–1625) Bishop of Winchester
Preces Privatae (ed. F. E. Brightman, 1903, pp. 48, 78, 273)

O Thou that art the hope of all the ends of the earth:
   remember all thy creation for good;
      O visit the world with thy compassions.
O Thou preserver of men, O Lord thou lover of man:
   remember all our race,
      and, as Thou hast concluded all in unbelief,
        on all have mercy, O Lord.
O Thou that for this end didst die and come to life again,
   that Thou mightest be Lord both of dead and living:
   Whether we live or whether we die we are thine,
      Thou art our Lord:
   have mercy on quick and dead, O Lord. . . .

Remember, O Lord God, all spirits and all flesh
   Whom we have remembered and whom we have not remembered,
   from righteous Abel unto this day that now is. . . .

Thou which art Lord at once of the living and of the dead;
   Whose are we whom the present world yet holdeth in the flesh
   Whose are they withal whom, unclothed of the body, the world to
      come hath even now received:
   give to the living mercy and grace
      to the dead rest and light perpetual;
   give to the Church truth and peace,
      to us sinners penitence and pardon.

15
Richard Field (1561–1616) Dean of Gloucester
Of the Church (1849 edn, vol. 1, p. 235; vol. 2, pp. 97f, 101)

If then the saints, for ought we know, do not see, know, and inter-meddle with our particular affairs, but pray only in general; there remaineth nothing else safely to be done by us, but to seek unto

God: and then, all these, both saints and angels, shall love us in him; and, what lieth in them, procure our good.

That it is lawful to pray for the acquittal and public remission of sins in the day of judgement, and the performing and perfecting of whatsoever is yet behind, there is no question that I know made by any: and I am well assured that in so doing, we exceedingly christianly express our love towards the departed, and give testimony of our persuasion that the souls of them that die do live; and that their bodies also shall be raised up at the last day: which thing, as Cassander saith truly, all the Christian Churches throughout the world, as well those of the East, as of the West, do and ever did; though they do not so certainly resolve what their state is that are departed hence; what is yet wanting unto them; or wherein or how far forth they may be benefited by our prayers; but the Romish conceit of purgatory, and their praying to deliver thence, none of the Eastern Churches admit, neither do we. . . .

From this, of prayer for the dead, let us come to the other objection, touching the commemoration of the blessed apostles, and other saints, and holy martyrs, by and through whose intercession, and for whose merits, the priest and people desireth God to grant that they may, in all things, be kept safe and strongly defended, by the help of the divine protection.

That the saints do pray for us *in genere*, desiring God to be merciful to us, and to do unto us whatsoever in any kind he knoweth needful for our good, there is no question made by us; and therefore this prayer[1] wherein the Church desireth God to be gracious to her, and to grant the things she desireth, the rather for that the saints in heaven also are suppliant for her, will not be found to contain any point of Romish doctrine disliked by us.

16
Thomas Morton (1564–1659) Bishop of Durham
A Catholic Appeal for Protestants, 2.8.6

In any doubtful matter it is presumption to believe, when there is no evident place of Scripture to resolve upon. Of which kind are both the Romish doctrine of purgatory and prayer for the dead: whereof we have neither precept nor promise nor direct example in the volume of God's book, no, not where purposely and at large there is a discoursing of the state of the dead. . . . Wherefore, seeing this Romish doctrine is found to have proceeded not from faith but from doubtfulness, nor from a direct and catholic consent but from prejudice, much less from the light of the divine testament, which is the direct line and level of all necessary truth: we are justly stayed from performing any such kindness, which instead of showing love unto the dead, might seduce the living with deceivable hopes of succour after their

[1] The Canon of the Latin Mass.

death; when it assureth the Church that all such as die in Christ are in blessed rest from their labours, but the wicked and such as die in their sins sink down to the lowest hell, as hopeless when dead to be relieved by the prayers of the living, as were those living [sc. Dives' brothers] helped by the prayers of that dead [sc. Dives himself].

17
Joseph Hall (1574–1656) Bishop of Norwich
Works (ed. Pratt, vol. 5, p. 442)

As for the practice of praying for the dead, there hath been of old some use of it, but not the Romish; that is, not with an intuition to their feigned Purgatory; for that in hand, Bellarmin hath stated it thus: The question is, What dead men are helped by our prayers? "It is certain", saith he, "that they profit not either the blessed or the damned souls; the former need them not, the latter cannot be aided by them". *Solum iis prosunt, qui sunt in purgatorio,* is his conclusion: and let them keep that breath to blow that fire. For us, we know that the blood of Jesus Christ is that, which purgeth us from all our sins: to that, shall be our only recourse. As for our prayers, let us bestow them upon the living: and let them be no other, when we refer to the dead, than the congratulations of their joys present; and the testimonies of our hope and desire of their future resurrection, and consummation of blessedness, together with all the glorious Saints of heaven.

18
Joseph Hall (1574–1656) Bishop of Norwich
The Old Religion (chap. 14)

But could the saints of heaven know our actions, yet our hearts they cannot. This is the peculiar skill of their Maker.... Yet, could they know our secretest desires, it is an honour that God challengeth as proper to himself, to be invoked in our prayers.... How absurd therefore is it in reason, when the King of heaven calls us to him, to run with our petitions to the guard or pages of the court!... Besides, how uncertain must our devotions needs be, when we can have no possible assurance of their audience! for who can know that a saint hears him? That God ever hears us, we are as sure, as we are unsure to be heard of saints. Nay, we are sure we cannot be all heard of them; for what finite nature can divide itself betwixt ten thousand suppliants, at one instant, in several regions of the world, much less impart itself whole to each? Either, therefore, we must turn the saints into so many deities, or we must yield that some of our prayers are unheard; and, "whatsoever is not of faith is sin".... The doctrine therefore and practice of the Romish invocation of saints, both as new and erroneous, against Scripture and reason, we have justly rejected, and are thereupon ejected as unjustly.

19

William Forbes (1585–1634) Bishop of Edinburgh
Considerationes Modestae (L.A.C.T., vol. 2, "Of Purgatory", pp. 89, 91, 95–7, 139–41 ; "Of the Intercession and Invocation of Angels and Saints", pp 229–31, 313)

Let us now speak of the prayers and offerings for the dead, by which Romanists think that their purgatory is very effectually proved.

But here first the opinion of some of the more rigid Protestants is to be condemned, who altogether disapprove of and condemn prayers for the dead, because no precept nor example of such prayers is to be read in the Canonical books, either of the Old or New Testament. Certainly, even those who disapprove of this custom most strongly dare not deny that this custom is a most ancient one, and one thoroughly received in the whole Church of Christ, that even in the public prayers of the Church, a commemoration should be made of the departed, and rest should be sought from God for those who have died piously and in the peace of the Church. . . .

Moreover this very ancient custom was full of piety. Most truly also Cassander writes: "in all Christian souls", he says "this hath ever been implanted, that they should commend to the mercy of God the spirits of those who, having been initiated with the sacrament of Christ, have departed from this life in the confession of his name, with some significance of penitence, that they should pray for their remission of sin, eternal rest, and fellowship with the elect. . . ." This most ancient and universal custom of the Church, very many of the most learned among Protestants even do not condemn. . . .

These most ancient and pious prayers[1] the Bishops of the Church of England afterwards expunged, at the suggestion and by the advice of Bucer and others ; or changed them into another form, I know not what, redolent of modern novelty. . . . Would to God, that the Church of England . . . had in this matter and in a few others rather conformed herself to the most ancient custom of the universal Church, than on account of the errors and abuses which little by little crept in afterwards, absolutely to have rejected and entirely to have abolished it, to the great scandal of almost all other Christians. . . .

Let not the custom of praying and offering for the dead, which is most ancient, and thoroughly received in the universal Church of Christ, almost from the very times of the Apostles, be any longer rejected by Protestants as being unlawful, or at least useless. Let them reverence the judgement of the ancient Church, and recognize a practice confirmed by the unbroken series of so many centuries, and in future religiously use both in public and in private this rite, though not as absolutely necessary or commended by the divine law, yet as lawful, and also useful, and always approved by the Church universal ; that so the peace so long desired by all truly learned and pious people may at length return to the Christian world. . . .

[1]Those of the 1549 Prayer Book.

The Church of England herself retains and practices to the present day, many rites received from the Fathers as lawful and pious, of which you cannot find either any precept or any example in Holy Scripture; as the sign of the cross on the forehead of the baptized, kneeling at receiving the Eucharist, the fast of Lent and other stated times of fasting, and many other such things, in spite of the reclamations of the Puritans continually objecting the precept, "Ye shall not add to that which I command you".... When a thing is merely indifferent, it is enough if it be not repugnant to Holy Scripture, but is agreeable to it. The Fathers "being led", to use the words of Cassander, "by the testimonies and examples of Scripture, from which it is evident that the prayers which just men offer for others are of great avail with God; and being moreover certainly persuaded that the righteous at their death do not cease to be, but joined to Christ, lead a blessed life", and that they pray for us more ardently than before, in as much as they are endued with greater love than formerly, and as Cyprian says, "are secure in their own immortality and anxious for our safety"—the Fathers, I say, desired very greatly that during their pilgrimage in this life they might be aided by the prayers of those who were reigning in heaven (a thing which no-one will say not to be lawful), and even asked it, so far, namely, as the saints have knowledge of our condition. For although it be altogether uncertain whether they have an *idiopatheia* (to use the expression of some Protestants), that is, a particular acquaintance with our necessities and distresses, yet who in their senses would deny to them a *sympatheia* or general knowledge derived from the Word of God and their own past experience? And the Fathers declared this their wish and desire, by calling upon, either all in general, or even some particular individuals by name, both in their public and their private prayers, as being present in spirit and soul. Not to constitute them propitiatory mediators with God in the highest sense, but that by their prayers, which they believed to be of great avail with God, joined also to their own prayers, they might the more easily obtain their desires from God the Father through Jesus Christ, the only Mediator and propitiator....

But to conclude at length this dissertation. Let God alone be religiously adored; let him alone be prayed to, through Christ who is the only and sole Mediator between God and man, truly and strictly speaking. Let not the very ancient custom received in the universal Church, as well Greek as Latin, of addressing angels and saints, in the manner we have described, be condemned or rejected as impious, nor indeed as vain and foolish by the more rigid Protestants. Let the foul abuses and superstitions which have crept in, be taken away. And so peace may thereafter be easily established and settled between the dissentient parties as regards this controversy. Which may the God of peace, and all godly concord vouchsafe to grant us for the sake of his only begotten Son.

20
John Bramhall (1594–1663) Archbishop of Armagh
The Answer to la Milletière (*Works*, L.A.C.T. vol. 1, pp. 59f)

It is a common fault of your writers always to couple Prayer for the dead and Purgation together, as if the one did necessarily impose or imply the other ; —in whose steps you tread. Prayer for the dead hath often proceeded upon mistaken grounds, often from true grounds, both inconsistent with your Purgatory. [Numerous views about the state of the departed held by the Fathers are described ; none corresponding exactly to the doctrine of Purgatory.] . . . Though the sins of the faithful be privately and particularly remitted at the day of death, yet the public promulgation of their pardon at the Day of Judgement is to come. Though their souls be always in an estate of blessedness, yet they want the consummation of this blessedness, extensively at least, until the body be re-united unto the soul ; and (as it is piously and probably believed) intensively also,—that the soul hath not yet so full and clear a vision of God, as it shall have hereafter. Then what forbids Christians to pray for this pubic acquittal, for this consummation of blessedness?—So we do pray, as often as we say, "Thy Kingdom come", or "Come Lord Jesus, come quickly". Our Church is yet plainer ; "that we, with this our brother and all other departed in the faith of thy Holy Name, may have our perfect consummation of blessedness in thy everlasting Kingdom".

21
John Bramhall (1594–1663) Archbishop of Armagh
Works (L.A.C.T., vol. 1, pp. 57ff ; see also vol. 2, p. 633)

If your Invocation of Saints were not such as it is . . . yet it is not necessary for two reasons: first, no Saint doth love us so well as Christ: . . . and, secondly, we have no command from God to invocate them . . . but we have another command, "Call upon Me in the day of trouble, and I will hear thee". We have no promise to be heard, when we do invocate them ; but we have another promise,—"Whatsoever ye shall ask the Father in My name, ye shall receive it". We have no example in Holy Scripture of any that did invocate them, but rather the contrary ;—"See thou do it not" ; "I am thy fellow-servant, worship God". We have no certainty that they do hear our particular prayers, especially mental prayers, yea, a thousand prayers poured out at one instant in several parts of the world.

22
Herbert Thorndike (1598–1672) Prebendary of Westminster
Of the Laws of the Church, Book 3 (*Works*, L.A.C.T., vol. 4, pp. 710, 722f, 762f)

It hath been a custom so general in the Church to pray for the dead, that no beginning of it can be assigned, no time, no part of the

Church, where it has not been used. And though the rejecting of it makes not Aerius a heretic, as disbelieving any part of the faith; yet, had he broke from the Church upon no other cause but that which the whole Church besides him owned, he must as a schismatic have gone into Epiphanius his list of heresies, intending to comprise all parties severed from the Church. . . .

It is manifest, that in the service appointed in the time of Edward the Sixth[1] prayer is made for the dead, both before the Communion, and at the Burial, to the same purpose as I maintain. It is manifest also, that it was changed in Queen Elizabeth's time, to content the Puritans, who now it appears could not be content with less than breaking of the Church in pieces.

And therefore, since unity hath not been obtained by parting with the law of the Catholic Church, . . . I continue the resolution to bound reformation by the rule of the Catholic Church; allowing, that it may be matter of reformation to restore the prayers which are made for the dead to the original sense of the whole Church; but maintaining that to take away all prayer for the dead is not paring off abuses but cutting to the quick. . . .

I must come to particulars, that I may be understood. He that could wish, that the memories of the martyrs, and other saints who lived so as to assure the Church they would have been martyrs had they been called to it, had not been honoured, as it is plain that they were honoured by Christians, must find in his heart by consequence to wish that Christianity had not prevailed. For this honour depending on nothing but the assurance of their happiness in them that remained alive, was that, which moved unbelievers to bethink themselves of the reason they had to be Christians. . . . Neither is it to be doubted, that the saints in happiness pray for the Church militant, and that they have knowledge thereof; if they go not out like sparkles, and are kindled again when they resume their bodies, which I have shewed our common Christianity allows not. For is it possible to imagine that knowing anything (that is, knowing God and themselves) they should not know, that God hath a Church in this world, upon the consummation whereof their consummation dependeth? Or is it possible that, knowing this . . . they should not intercede with God for the consummation of it, and the means thereof?

23
Herbert Thorndike (1598–1672) Prebendary of Westminster
Just Weights and Measures (Works, L.A.C.T., vol. 5, pp. 248f)

But I must by no means leave this place, till I have paid the debt which I owe to the opinion which I have premised; and openly profess again and again, that we "weigh not by our own weights, nor mete by our own measures", if, believing one Catholic Church, and

[1]1549.

enjoying episcopacy and the Church-lands upon that account, we recall not the memorial of the dead, as well as the living into this service.[1] There is the same ground to believe the communion of saints in the prayers, which those that depart in the highest favour with God make for us, in the prayers which we make for those that depart in the lowest degree of favour with God, that there is for the common Christianity; namely, the Scriptures interpreted by the perpetual practice of God's Church. Therefore there is ground enough for the faith of all Christians, that those prayers are accepted, which desire God to hear the saints for us, to send the deceased in Christ rest and peace and light and refreshment and a good trial at the day of judgement and accomplishment of happiness after the same. And seeing the abating of the first form under Edward VI hath wrought no effect, but to give them that desired it an appetite to root up the whole; what thanks can we render to God for escaping so great a danger, but by sticking to a rule, that will stick firm to us, and carry us through any dispute in religion, and land us in the haven of a quiet conscience; what troubles soever we may pass through in maintaining, that the reformation of the Church will never be according to the rule which it ought to follow, till it cleave to the catholic Church of Christ in this particular.

24

John Pearson (1638–1686) Bishop of Chester
Exposition of the Creed (art. 9, chap. 2) (1847 edn, by E. Barton, vol. 1, pp. 422–3)

The mystical union between Christ and his Church, the spiritual conjunction of the members to the Head, is the true foundation of that communion which one member hath with another, all the members living and increasing by the same influence which they receive from him. But death, which is nothing else but the separation of the soul from the body, maketh no separation in the mystical union, no breach of the spiritual conjunction, and consequently there must continue the same communion, because there remaineth the same foundation....

This communion of the saints in heaven and earth, upon the mystical union of Christ their head, being fundamental and internal, what acts or external operations it produceth, is not so certain. That we communicate with them in hope of that happiness which they actually enjoy is evident; that we have the Spirit of God given us as an earnest, and so a part of their felicity, is certain. But what they do in heaven in relation to us on earth particularly considered, or what we ought to perform in reference to them in heaven, beside a reverential respect, and study of imitation, is not revealed unto us in the Scriptures, nor can be concluded by necessary deduction from any principles of Christianity. They which first found this part of the

[1]The Holy Communion.

F

article in the Creed,[1] and delivered their exposition unto us, have made no greater enlargement of this communion, as to the saints of heaven, than the society of hope, esteem, and imitation on our side, of desires and supplications on their side; and what is now taught by the Church of Rome is, as an unwarrantable, so a novitious interpretation.

25
Thomas Ken (1637–1711) Bishop of Bath and Wells
Funeral Sermon for Lady Margaret Mainard (*The Prose Works,* ed. W. Benham, 1889, p. 65)

But why did I call her death a loss? It is rather a gain; we were all travelling the same way, as pilgrims towards our heavenly country, she had only got the start of us, and is gone before, and is happy first, and I am persuaded that we still enjoy her prayers for us above, however I am sure that we enjoy her good works here below, which now appear more illustrious, and without that veil her modesty and her humility cast over them.

26
Thomas Ken (1637–1711) Bishop of Bath and Wells
An Exposition of the Church Catechism (ibid., p. 140)

I believe, O most holy Jesu, that thy saints here below have communion with thy saints above, they praying for us in heaven, we here on earth celebrating their memories, rejoicing at their bliss, giving thee thanks for their labours of love, and imitating their examples; for which all love, all glory be to thee.

27
Thomas Wilson (1663–1755) Bishop of Sodor and Man
Maxims of Piety and Morality (*Works,* L.A.C.T., vol. 5, pp. 395–6)

225. *Bp Barrow's Epitaph.* Exuviae Is. Episcopi Asaphensis in manum Domini depositae, in spem laetae Resurrectionis per sola Christi merita.

O vos transeuntes in Domum Domini, Domum Orationis, orate pro conservo vestro, ut inveniat requiem, in die Domini.

Mr Thorndike's Epit. Tu, Lector, Requiem ei et beatam in Xto. Resurrectionem precare. . . .

228. *Mediator.* Christ yᵉ only M. of Redemption, all Christians (even the Saints departed) may be M. of intercession, one for another.

28
Thomas Wilson (1663–1755) Bishop of Sodor and Man
Collectanae (ibid. vol. 7, p. 239)

Grant unto them, I beseech thee, thy mercy and everlasting peace, and

[1] The Communion of Saints.

that at the great day I and they and all who are of the mystical Body of thy Son may be set on his right hand, and hear that his most joyful word, "Come ye blessed", etc.

Grant them peace in the mansions of the blessed, who are departed and are at rest in Christ.

29
William Nicholls (1664–1712)
A Comment on the Book of Common Prayer (1710 edn, additional notes, p. 64)

I take the liberty to observe, that prayer for the dead is not countenanced . . . by the Church of England; for she has taken effectual care, to leave out every thing which may give any umbrage thereunto, in all her publick Books and Offices. . . . Indeed it must be said, that our Church has not openly condemned prayer for the dead, in the commemorative way of the ancients, nor a desire of the improvement of the bliss of pious souls, and that all faithful persons may find mercy at the final judgement (out of regard to those venerable persons who practised the same) as she has done the popish doctrine of purgatory; so that men are at liberty to hold it as a private theological opinion . . . without blame; but they are not authorized to preach it to the people, there being no ground for it in Scripture, nor from the authentick Books of our national Church, which is so far from recommending it, that for 150 years past she has plainly discountenanced it.

30
Samuel Johnson (1709–84) Author
Prayers and Meditations Composed by Samuel Johnson, LL. D. (ed. H. E. Savage, 1927, pp. 12, 12, 121)

(Easter 1753) And, O Lord, so far as it may be lawful for me, I commend to thy fatherly goodness the soul of my departed wife; beseeching thee to grant her whatever is best in her present state and finally to receive her to eternal happiness. All this I beg for Jesus Christ's sake, whose death I am now about to commemorate.

(23 Jan 1759) I commend, O Lord, so far as it may be lawful, into thy hands, the soul of my departed mother, beseeching thee to grant her whatever is most beneficial to her in her present state.

(6 September 1783, on the death of Anna Williams) Almighty and most merciful Father, who art the Lord of life and death, who givest and who takest away, teach me to adore thy providence. Whatsoever thou shalt allot me, make me to remember with due thankfulness the comforts which I have received from my friendship with Anna Williams. Look upon her, O Lord, with mercy, and prepare me, by thy grace, to die with hope, and to pass by death to eternal happiness, through Jesus Christ our Lord.

31
Samuel Johnson (1709–84) Author
Life by Boswell (ed. G. B. Hill, vol. 2, p. 255)

Toplady. Does not their[1] invocation of saints suppose omnipresence in the saints?

Johnson. No, Sir; it supposes only pluri-presence; and when spirits are divested of matter, it seems probable that they should see with more extent than when in an embodied state. There is, therefore, no approach to an invasion of any of the divine attributes, in the invocation of saints. But I think it is will-worship, and presumption. I see no command for it, and therefore think it is safer not to practise it.

32
G. S. Faber (1773–1854) Master of Sherburn Hospital, Durham
The Primitive Doctrine of Justification Investigated (2nd edn, Seeley and Burnside, 1839, pp. 432, 439)

The truth is, the Church of England, whether influenced or not influenced by others, stood pledged, by her own decision, to throw out those prayers for the dead.[2] Unless wholly regardless of consistency, it was impossible for her to retain, at once, both such prayers and her own sixth Article. The sixth Article propounds: that, "Whatever is not read in Holy Scripture, nor may be proved thereby, is not to be required of any man, that it should be believed as an article of the faith." Now, if prayers for the dead had remained authoritatively fixed in the Anglican liturgy, it is quite clear that, by an imperative injunction of their use, a doctrine which is neither read in Scripture nor may be proved thereby, the doctrine, to wit, of *the bounden duty and certain benefit of praying for the dead,* would, to all intents and purposes have been imposed upon the belief of her members, as an article of the faith. . . . Those who, on the ill-disguised principle of the Roman Church, patronise the imposition of *liturgical prayers for the dead,* under whatever aspect, most indisputably take the first step into popery.

33
Reginald Heber (1783–1826) Bishop of Calcutta
Correspondence with Frances Williams Wynn, in *Diaries of a Lady of Quality,* ed. A. Hayward (London 1864), pp. 208f; quoted in J. Wickham Legg, *English Church Life from the Restoration to the Tractarian Movement* (1914), p. 332.

Few persons, I believe, have lost a beloved object, more particularly by *sudden* death, without feeling an earnest desire to commend them in their prayers to God's mercy, and a sort of instinctive impression

[1]The Roman Catholics'.
[2]Those in the 1549 Prayer Book.

that such devotions might still be serviceable to them in the intermediate state which we are taught by Scripture precedes the final
judgement. The Roman Catholics, by their interested doctrines of hired
masses for the dead, and by their unwarranted and melancholy notion
of a purgatory to which even the good are liable, have prejudiced
the greater number of Protestants against this opinion; and it is, I
confess, one which is not so clearly revealed or countenanced in
Scripture, as to make the practice of praying for the dead obligatory
on any Christian....

I have accordingly been myself in the habit for some years of
recommending on some occasions, as after receiving the Sacrament,
etc., my lost friends to God's goodness and compassion through his
Son, as what can do them no harm, and *may,* and I hope *will,* be of
service to them. Only this caution I always endeavour to observe—
that I beg his forgiveness at the same time praying for myself if
unknowingly I am too presumptuous.

34
E. B. Pusey (1800–82) Regius Professor at Oxford
Eleven Addresses to the Companions of the Love of Jesus (1868,
pp. 126, 127, 134)

But we have no doubt that we *may* pray. For the whole Church so
prayed, much nearer to the time when the beloved disciple left this
earth, than many of us are to the early memories of our fathers. And
however, in evil days, the public and ritual use of those prayers was
laid aside in the Church of England, yet even a Court of Ecclesiastical
Law formally decided their lawfulness, according to the doctrine and
discipline of the Church of England, and the departed are but in-
distinctly yet *are* included in our Eucharistic prayer, "by the merits
and death of thy Son Jesus Christ and through faith in his blood,
we and *all thy whole Church* may obtain remission of our sins and
all other benefits of his passion"....

I say this, in case any should be afraid so to pray. But since it is
lawful, what an unspeakable privilege! It is so cold a thought that we
have for the time no more to do with those who loved us here, and
whom we loved, that it must needs, on that ground alone, be false,
because it is so contrary to love. And yet much more, since the Church
has always prayed for the departed from the very first! It belongs
to the Communion of Saints, that they, in the attainment of certain
salvation and incapable of a thought other than according to the
mind of God and filled with his love, shall pray and long for us
who are still on the stormy sea of this world, our salvation still un-
secured: and that we, on our side, should pray for such things, as God
in his goodness wills to bestow on them....

The love of the departed avails for us, in gaining grace for us in
this our perilous voyage.... Our prayers avail for them to abridge

the time of their waiting. So would God perpetuate divine love beyond the grave; so would he, in the communion of saints, provide that "they without us, should not be made perfect", that they who have attained, should be yet indebted to our love, while we are yet more indebted to their love. For they are in certain possession of the bliss of eternity, even though its fruition is for a time delayed; we are still tossed upon this boisterous sea where so many around us are alas! for ever shipwrecked, and where he alone, to whom they pray, can bring us safe to the shore.

35
E. M. Goulburn (1818–97) Dean of Norwich
The Office of the Holy Communion in the Book of Common Prayer (4th edn, Rivingtons, 1865, pp. 145f)

Such are the feelings and instincts of nature towards our departed friends. Like all our instincts, they may lead us astray. Very early in the history of the Church they began to lead Christians astray. Very early pure religion began to be flawed and marred by too strong an ingredient of the sentimental. Prayers for the dead crept into the early liturgies—not indeed forbidden by God's Word, but nowhere commanded, and because not commanded, therefore surely at best questionable. But worse was still behind, for which this beginning paved the way.... Thanksgiving, however, for the righteous dead, and prayer for grace to follow their example, is a thing wholly different in kind from intercession for them; and as soon as the Reformation was firmly established, it was thought not only safe, but desirable, to add to the Prayer for the Church Militant the clause which commemorates the departed righteous.

36
T. P. Boultbee (1818–84) Principal, London College of Divinity
A Commentary on the Thirty-nine Articles (9th edn, Longmans, Green and Co., 1893, p. 192)

But when such questions as those noted in the present Article[1] are raised, the silence of Scripture is conclusive. It would be simply impossible for the writers of the Epistles to have omitted directions about prayers for the dead, notices of purgatory, and invocation of saints, if these had been any part of their system. No theory of "economy" or "reserve" can account for so extraordinary an omission. The Epistles often touch on the state of the departed, and are, above measure, copious on the subjects and nature of prayer; yet these things are omitted precisely where no Romish divine could avoid giving them the foremost place. The inference is as strong as it is obvious.

[1]Article XXII.

37
William Bright (1824–1901) Regius Professor at Oxford
Collect quoted in the *Cuddesdon Office Book* (1962), p. 180

O God, who hast brought us near to an innumerable company of angels, and to the spirits of just men made perfect ; grant us during our earthly pilgrimage to abide in their fellowship, and in our heavenly country to become partakers of their joy.

38
H. P. Liddon (1829–90) Canon of St Paul's
Collect quoted in the *Cuddesdon Office Book* (1962), p. 180

O God, the Maker and Redeemer of all believers, grant to all thy servants a merciful judgement at the last day ; that in the face of all thy creatures, they may be acknowledged as thy true children ; through Jesus Christ, thine only Son our Lord.

39
H. B. Swete (1835–1917) Regius Professor at Cambridge
The Holy Catholic Church: The Communion of Saints. A study in the Apostles' Creed (1915), pp. 219f, 243f, 230.

Thus, with much variety of detail, the great Christian teachers of the second and third centuries were generally agreed in regarding the dead in Christ as expecting the Resurrection in a state intermediate between earth and heaven, receiving already in part the reward of their faith, but looking for its completion at the Coming of the Lord. Some of these writers add that Christian souls meanwhile undergo discipline, if discipline is necessary, or carry on their education for the higher life, receiving additions to their knowledge ; and as their nature grows and ripens under this process, rising to greater heights, and drawing nearer to the fulness of their joy. If some of these early teachers of the Church represented the discipline of souls under the image of fire, it was not the fire of penal suffering to which the figure pointed, but the refining fire of the Spirit, who would thus continue and complete in the saints the work of purification which he had begun on earth.

Prayer is our chief means of fellowship with fellow Christians who are separated from us by long distances. Our brethren in other lands across the sea pray for us, and we for them ; and this interchange of prayer is a bond which links together the members of Christ throughout the world.

If death does not involve a suspension of conscious life, there seems to be no reason why this kind of fellowship should not exist between the living and the departed. It is natural to suppose that departed Saints remember in their prayers those whom they knew on earth and that those who are still on earth can return the benefit. . . .

The intercession of the Saints at rest is a legitimate and necessary consequence of the fellowship in prayer which unites the whole Body of Christ. The invocation of the departed Saints is a practice based upon this truth, which is neither primitive, nor universal, and which has been found to be dangerous. It is earnestly to be hoped that no false sentiment may lead members of the English Church who realise the need of closer communion with the holy dead to fall back upon so precarious a way of attaining it. . . .

It is thus left open to members of the English Church to exercise their discretion in this matter [*sc.* of praying for the departed] at their private devotions at home or in Church, and there is evidence that this liberty has been used by some of the wisest and best sons of the Church from the beginning of the seventeenth century onwards. At the present day it is used by a large minority, or perhaps even a majority of well-instructed Churchmen, who at the same time loyally acquiesce in the exclusion of prayers for the departed from the authorised forms of public worship until such time as it shall please God to restore them to us.

40
C. H. H. Wright (1836–1909) Theologian, Clerical Superintendent, the Protestant Reformation Society
The Intermediate State and Prayers for the Dead (Nisbet, 1900), p. xvi

Prayers for the dead under such circumstances soon passed away. As revived in our Church today, they certainly lead to the re-introduction of masses for the dead. They lead up distinctly to a belief in purgatory, which is plainly avowed by not a few, and those who now claim some consideration for their weakness, are certain after a little to assume a different tone, and speak of the cruelty of those who refuse to offer up prayers for the dead. The solemn duty of resisting an error in its commencement should be more often insisted on, for the admission of any practice not based on the teaching of Holy Scripture is certain to lead ultimately to grievous doctrinal departures from the faith.

41
H. C. G. Moule (1841–1920) Bishop of Durham
Christus Consolator (S.P.C.K., 1915), pp. 96–8

Upon the grave and tender problem of prayer for the departed, the Bible, so I venture to think, after long reflection, is absolutely reserved. I cannot think, therefore, that the warrant for such prayer is a fact of revelation. Christians who so pray should have a reverent regard, when there is any occasion for such a feeling, for the misgivings of others, in whom, very probably, the thought of spiritual communion with their vanished ones is just as strong and warm as in themselves, and who continually greet them in the Lord, reaching them in Him through the veil. Only, they do not see the warrant for intercessory prayer for them.

They do think, perhaps, and most justly, that at least the too easy use of such prayer may tend *to muffle* the divine appeals to man to seek salvation today.

Misgivings about prayer for the dead are wholly justified, if the prayer in question means necessarily prayer for deliverance from gloom and pain, rather than a breath of loving aspiration sent after the spirit into its abode of light, asking as a certainty may be asked for, for the perpetual growth in the emancipated being of the graces and bliss of the heavenly rest, and its holy progress and education in the knowledge of its Lord. It is undoubted that such prayer for the departed is found in the fragmentary remains of very early Christian literature, certainly within half a century of the last apostles. Never there, nor ever in the inscriptions of the Roman catacombs, I think, does it suggest a purgatorial belief. It might almost be said to be, as regards its spirit, as much salutation and aspiration as petition. But in form it is prayer. And I for one cannot condemn such exercises of the soul, where reverent thought invites to it, in the private devotions of a Christian.

42
William Temple (1881–1944) Archbishop of Canterbury
Essay on "The Church" in *Foundations,* ed. B. H. Streeter, 1910, pp. 343, 346f

The Catholic Church is universal not only in space but in time; the living and the dead alike are members of it. "The gates of Hades shall not prevail against it." Death is no ultimate division in that society. . . . Indeed, we who are united by faith to Christ, are even now, as St Paul declares, in heaven. . . .

As in the Incarnation, so in the Eucharist. He comes unto his own, and only because he comes to us can we be sure that we may approach him. It is all his doing, not ours. He gives, and we receive; when we approach it is because he draws us. But the realm to which he draws us is not merely the sanctuary of a Church, nor an Upper Chamber in Jesusalem; it is the presence of God Almighty, where he is worshipped by the heavenly host with hymns that are never silent, and thanksgivings that never cease.

For "we are not come to a mount that may be touched" nor to an altar that may be seen with bodily eyes, "but we are come . . . to innumerable hosts of angels, to the general assembly and church of the first-born . . . and to God the Judge of all, and to the spirits of just men made perfect, and to Jesus" (Heb. 12, vv 18, 22).

Thus the one great "Service" of the Christian Church emphasizes the true nature of the Church. We have lost sight of a great part of this truth in England, Abuses and errors had become associated with parts of the full doctrine, and in the abolition of the abuses the truth itself suffered. Prayers for the dead dropped out of use; but they represent a spontaneous and generous impulse of the human heart, and the right to offer them is implicit in the doctrine of the Communion of Saints. The invocation of Saints passed out of use, because men not only asked the Saints to present their prayers, but prayed to the Saints instead of God; but if "with Angels and Archangels and with all the company of Heaven we laud and magnify God's glorious Name", why should we not ask that company to assist our prayers as much as our praises?

43
William Temple (1881–1944) Archbishop of Canterbury
Fellowship with God (1920), pp. 78f

Let us pray for those whom we know and love who have passed on to the other life. The objection to prayers for the dead rests on two assumptions, one of them unfounded and the other definitely false. The first is the assumption that at death all is irrevocably settled; whatever be the state of the soul at that moment, in that state it must unalterably remain. Neither in revelation, nor in reason is there a shred of evidence for this once prevalent delusion. We cannot doubt that growth in grace and power and love continues after death. The other assumption which leads men to object to prayers for the dead is the belief that we should only pray for such blessings as we fear may not be granted unless we pray for them. But this is flatly contradictory to the teaching of Christ. We are to pray for all good things because it is our Father's will to give them, and we should acknowledge that we receive all good things at his hand. We do not pray for them because God will otherwise neglect them. We pray for them because we know he loves and cares for them, and we claim the privilege of uniting our love for them with God's.

But do not be content to pray for them. Let us also ask them to pray for us. In such prayers while they lived on earth they both displayed and consecrated their love towards us. Doubtless that ministry of love continues; but let us seek it, ask for it, claim it. It is in the mutual service of prayer, our prayer for them and theirs for us, that we come closest to them. "For our fellowship with them is in Christ", and we find them when we seek them in his Name.

44
Alan Paton (1903–   ) Author
Kontakion for You Departed (1969, pp. 67–70; a book written after the death of his wife)

I rang Sister Elspeth the other afternoon and I reminded her that she had said that you would be interceding for me. I asked her what theological justification she had for such a statement, and when she said she did not know, I suggested she asked Reverend Mother. What came back to me was not an answer to my question at all, but one of the most remarkable prayers that I have ever read:

"O God, the God of the spirits of all flesh, in whose embrace all creatures live, in whatsoever world or condition they be: I beseech thee for her whose name and dwelling-place and every need thou knowest. Lord, vouchsafe her light and rest, peace and refreshment, joy and consolation in Paradise, in the companionship of saints, in the presence of Christ, in the ample folds of thy great love.

Grant that her life may unfold itself in thy sight, and find a sweet employment in the spacious fields of eternity. If she hath ever been hurt or maimed by any unhappy word or deed of mine, I pray thee of thy great pity to heal and restore her, that she may serve thee without hindrance.

Tell her, O gracious Lord, if it may be, how much I love her and miss her and long to see her again; and if there be ways in which she may come, vouchsafe her to me as a guide and guard and grant me a sense of her nearness as thy laws permit.

If in aught I can minister to her peace, be pleased of thy love to let this be; and mercifully keep me from every act which may deprive me of the sight of her as soon as our trial time is over, or mar the fulness of our joy when the end of the day hath come.

Pardon, O gracious Lord and Father, whatsoever is amiss in this prayer, and let thy will be done, for my will is blind and erring, but thine is able to do exceeding abundantly above all that we ask or think, through Jesus Christ our Lord. Amen."

This prayer is based on many tremendous assumptions. One is that the one departed is in God's embrace, in Paradise, in the presence of Christ and the companionship of the saints. A second is that she lives, and that her life is being lived to some purpose. A third is that God, *if it may be,* may tell her that she is loved and missed, and, *if there be ways,* may give her to the one who loves and misses her, as a guard and guide, and may allow her nearness to be felt, *if His laws permit.* A fourth assumption is that she and the one who prays for her will be reunited, and the one who prays for her will *see* her, if he does nothing that may deprive him of such a fulfilment. Therefore the one who prays, aware no doubt of a magnitude of his assumptions, asks to be pardoned whatever is amiss in this his prayer.

Although I myself am aware of the magnitude of these assumptions, and although I believe that not one of them can be held except in faith, yet I can pray this prayer with all my being. My whole being responds to it. . . .

Therefore I shall pray this prayer for you with all my being. Never could I have made a prayer for myself so humble and so trusting. . . .

"If she has ever been hurt or maimed by an unhappy word or deed of mine, I pray thee of thy great mercy to heal and restore her, that she may serve thee without hindrance."

I do not think you were ever maimed by any word or deed of mine. You lived too warm and full a life to be maimed. But for the times that I hurt you, may I be forgiven. I cannot remember that we ever went to bed in anger but if we did, may I be forgiven for that also.